Irish Baby Names

Irish Baby Names

Mairéad Byrne

foulsham
LONDON • NEW YORK • TORONTO • SYDNEY

foulsham

The Publishing House, Bennetts Close, Cippenham,
Slough, Berkshire, SL1 5AP, England

Foulsham books can be found in all good bookshops and direct from
www.foulsham.com

ISBN 13: 978-0-572-03176-3
ISBN 10: 0-572-03176-9

Copyright © 2006 W. Foulsham & Co. Ltd

Cover photograph © Superstock

A CIP record for this book is available from the British Library

Printed in Great Britain by Cox & Wyman Ltd, Reading, Berkshire

Contents

Introduction

The Irish have always been great travellers, so their names, like the people, have spread throughout the world. Today, Irish names – as all things Irish – are enjoying enormous popularity.

This book offers you a choice of 300 Irish names for your new baby: 150 each for boys and girls. You'll find the most popular current choices (in 2005 the top five for girls were Siobhan, Aisling, Deirdre, Niamh and Eileen, and for boys, Aidan, Liam, Declan, Ciarán and Conor), along with lots of very old names and many unusual ones.

In Ireland, many names are used for both sexes, with surnames often used as first names too.

Far more Irish boys' names exist than girls', reflecting the fact that Ireland was a patriarchal society, and most historical records are concerned with the activities of men not women.

Making your choice

Many Irish names have several different spellings, which have been moulded and adapted by history. To make it as easy as possible to choose, we have listed girls' and boys' names in alphabetical order, under the most commonly used form of the name, with information on the meaning and background of each.

Where applicable, we've also given alternative spellings, including the Gaelic form if it's different, other older forms and the anglicised version if there is one. In some cases, the anglicised spelling is now the most commonly used form.

So you'll often find that not only do you have a choice of name, but a choice of the form too. You may prefer the spelling and sound of an older version of a name to the contemporary one. You're spoiled for choice!

Where do Irish names come from?

Irish names reflect the country's turbulent history. Over 12,000 Irish names were recorded in early sources, with thousands falling out of use in the Middle Ages. Many were introduced into Ireland by invaders, with the Irish adopting the names and finding their own forms.

Some have Celtic origins: the Celts – or Gaels – arrived from about 700 BC onwards, bringing the Gaelic language to Ireland. Other names came in with the Norse invaders – the Vikings – in the ninth and tenth centuries.

Christianity, which was brought to Ireland by St Patrick in the fifth century, is also a source: names with Christian and Hebrew origins remain popular. Others are drawn from Latin, Greek and the Teutonic languages.

Many are saints' names. The Irish have hundreds of saints, and some children are given the name of the saint on whose feast day they're born or baptised. Others are the names of Irish heroes or historical figures.

Most names, however, came from the French and then the English invaders (the Anglo-Normans) from the twelfth to the fourteenth century; many of the English names had Saxon and Germanic origins. These Anglo-Norman names almost entirely supplanted the old Gaelic ones.

The process continued under the Tudor and Stuart settlements and under Cromwellian rule and colonisation in the seventeenth century. As English became the dominant language, particularly in the nineteenth century, English, biblical and classical names replaced indigenous Irish ones.

However, the Gaelic revival, in the late nineteenth and early twentieth centuries, saw a return to fashion of many old names drawn from Gaelic myths, legends and folklore.

Some names are so well travelled (e.g. Brian, Sheila) that the original Irish source of the name has almost been forgotten. Others have become so international (e.g. Kevin) that the modern anglicised spelling has taken on a life of its own, apart from its original Gaelic form (Caoimhín).

The influence of mass media (television, radio and the internet), along with cheap travel and mass tourism, are also factors. The world gets ever smaller, with Irish names exported worldwide and new names from other parts of the world added to the 'Irish collection' all the time. The popularity of some of these new names may endure; others may vanish as quickly as they arrived – in some cases, mercifully.

Why choose an Irish name?

Many factors influence parents in their choice of name. They may want to continue a family tradition, by giving a child a relative's name, often a grandparent, or one traditionally used in their family.

Those with an Irish background may choose a name that reflects their heritage: their patriotism for Ireland and its history.

Parents' own religion may be a factor: some names are specific to Catholic families, and Catholics often name their children after a pope.

There's also a current revival of interest in old Irish names, in names of historical figures who became saints and in names from Celtic mythology. You may find yourself so beguiled by the stories from Celtic myth and legend that you want to find out more. Plenty of websites carry information on the most famous Irish epic stories; www.babynamesof ireland.com is one of the best.

Fashion and changes in taste are also deciding factors. The current popularity of Irish names is just one manifestation of the vogue for all things Irish over the last 15 years or so, from theatre to tourism. The Celtic economic tiger is still roaring. Since the late 1980s it has changed Ireland – and the attitudes of the rest of the world to Ireland – out of all recognition.

The rich and expressive meanings of Irish names also account for their popularity. You can, if you wish, name your child according to the colour of their hair or their skin (dark, fair or red, for example); after flowers, trees, animals or birds; or after their individual qualities. Whatever your baby's looks or character, you'll find a name to fit.

Finally, the attractive nature of an Irish name is often reason enough to choose it. Whether you have Irish connections or not, the older forms, including the Gaelic, have poetry in them: they sound and look just beautiful.

Please note:

1. In the information provided with each name the form *mac Néill* means 'son of Niall'; *Mac Neill* is the Irish surname; *MacNeill* is the anglicised surname.
2. All dates are AD, unless stated otherwise.

Irish Gaelic

Gaelic is a Celtic language, part of the Indo-European family of languages. There are several types: Irish Gaelic, Scottish Gaelic, and Manx form one group; Welsh, Cornish and Breton another. Irish Gaelic is usually just referred to as Irish, and we have followed this convention here.

Until the seventeenth century, Irish Gaelic (pronounced 'Gallic') was spoken by the whole Irish population. By the nineteenth century, the dominance of English had almost made it extinct. There was a Gaelic revival at the end of the nineteenth century and the beginning of the twentieth, however, and again after the formation of the Irish Free State in the south in 1922. A standard written form of Irish Gaelic was instituted in 1945.

Today about 500,000 people speak Irish, about one-seventh of the population of the Republic of Ireland. Irish Gaelic is the official language, but English has become the primary spoken language. However, the government has set up revival programmes for Irish Gaelic and it is now taught in all Irish schools.

The Irish alphabet has only 18 letters (13 consonants and 5 vowels), compared to 26 in English. The remaining letters appear in words that have been borrowed from other languages, but are not used in Irish Gaelic words.

Some Irish words resemble English ones, but have a very different meaning: *bean* means 'woman', *fear* means 'man', *bád* means 'boat'. Unlike English words, Irish words also have a gender, as in French or Italian, but it is not always logical: *cailín* ('girl') is masculine and *bean* ('woman') is feminine.

Spelling and pronunciation

Many Irish names have so many different spellings (they were recorded in Latin, French or English as well as Irish) that it's impossible to be definitive. Just choose the spelling you prefer.

Similarly, pronunciation of the Irish form of names is a minefield for non-Gaelic speakers. Words are not pronounced phonetically and there are many differences in dialect.

There are three main dialects in the south of Ireland: Munster (Cork and Kerry), Connacht (Connemara) and Ulster (Donegal). Within these there are also many local differences, giving varied pronunciation even for names as common as Sean and Deirdre, so it's impossible to give definitive guidance. The best advice is to ask a good local speaker of Irish.

The short pronunciation guide below will give you some general rules, however, though there are many exceptions to the rules.

Pronunciation guide
Vowels
Irish vowels are either long or short. Long vowels are marked with an acute accent, called a *fada* in Irish, which means 'long'.

In Irish names the stress is strong and usually falls on the first syllable. Vowels in later syllables are pronounced very lightly, unless they are accented and therefore pronounced long.

Short vowels (no accent)
Pronounce these as:

a	as English O as in *pot*
e	as English E as in *pet* (except when it comes before A, when it is silent)
i	as English I as in *pit* (some exceptions)
o	as English U as in *smut*
u	as English U as in *pull*

Long vowels (with accent)
Pronounce these as:

á	as English AW as in *call* (e.g. Siobhán)
é	as English AY as in *came*
í	as English EE as in *see*

ó	as English O as in *sow*
ú	as English OO as in *too*

Vowel combinations
Pronounce these as:

ei	as English I as in *vine*
ow	as English OW as in *owl*

Consonants
Irish Gaelic has only 13 consonants (B, C, D, F, G, H, L, M, N, P, R, S, T), fewer than English, and most are pronounced very much like English.

Consonants are either palatal, pronounced by raising the front of the tongue towards the hard palate (the roof of the mouth), or non-palatal, so pronounce:

c and g	always hard (as English *came* and *game*)
s	as SH before e or i (e.g. *Sean*: pronounced Shawn)
sh	as H
th	as H
bh, mh	as V (sometimes as W)
dh, fh and gh	usually silent (e.g. *Laoghaire*: pronounced Leary)
ch	as guttural K (e.g. Scottish *loch*)

Broad and slender
Irish vowels can either be broad (a, o, u and á, ó, ú) or slender (e, i and é, í).

Irish consonants are also broad or slender. Broad consonants are preceded or followed by a broad vowel (a, o, u or á, ó ú) and are non-palatal. Slender consonants are preceded or followed by a slender vowel (e, i or é, í) and are palatal.

11

Girls' names A to Z

Key to names

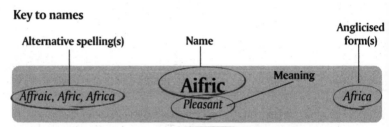

Alternative spelling(s)   Name   Anglicised form(s)

Affraic, Afric, Africa   **Aifric**   Meaning   *Africa*

Pleasant

The name of two eighth- and ninth-century abbesses of Kildare, who died in 738 and 833 respectively. This may be a Gaelic name, taken from the word for 'pleasant', or it may come from the name of the continent. One namesake was the daughter of Godred, king of the Isle of Man, and wife of John de Courcy. She founded the Cistercian Grey Abbey in the Ards, Co. Down.

Description

Abaigeal
Father of joy, joyfulness   *Abigail*

The name of the wife of the biblical King David, who was renowned for her prudence and beauty. It was a very common name in Ireland in the nineteenth century, particularly in the form Abaigh. In the south it was used as a genteel form of the Irish name Gobnait.

Aibreann
Aibrean   *April*

Aibreann is the word for April in the Irish language, so it would be a perfect name for a baby girl born in that month.

Aifric
Affraic, Afric, Africa   *Pleasant*   *Africa*

The name of two eighth- and ninth-century abbesses of Kildare, who died in 738 and 833 respectively. This may be a Gaelic name, taken from the word for 'pleasant', or it may come from the name of the continent. One namesake was the daughter of Godred, king of the Isle of Man, and wife of John de Courcy. She founded the Cistercian Grey Abbey in the Ards, Co. Down.

Ailbhe
Ailbe   *White, fair*   *Olive*

A famous bearer of the name was Ailbhe Grúadbrecc, which means 'freckled cheeks'. She was the daughter of Cormac mac Airt. Cailte, a warrior of the Fianna, a warrior band of about 150 chieftains and 4,000 warriors, musicians, poets, priests and physicians, claimed she was 'one of the four best women of her time that ever lay with a man'. She became the mistress of Fionn mac Cumhail, founder and leader of the Fianna, and Ireland's most important mythological hero, when she answered a series of riddles correctly.

13

Ailis

Ailís, Alish

Noble, well-born

Alice, Alicia

A name introduced into Ireland by the Normans in the French form Aliz; the Irish found their own form. It was the name of a notorious fourteenth-century witch from Kilkenny. Alice the Beautiful, a contemporary of King Arthur, had her face covered by a veil so people would not die at the sight of her beauty.

Áine

Radiance, splendour, brilliance

Enya

Áine was the goddess of love and fertility and the daughter of the foster son of the sea god Lir. The kings of Munster claimed her as an ancestor, as did the later Norman family, the FitzGeralds. In the Finn tales, she is one of the wives of Fionn mac Cumhail, Ireland's great mythological hero. Her name occurs in folklore all over Ireland: in Teelin, Co. Donegal, a hill called Cnoc Áine was associated with a mysterious piper and was considered dangerous for young girls. The name was once also used as a male name, but is now exclusively female.

Aingeal

Messenger

Angela

A name with a biblical connection, it is the Irish form of 'angel' from the Greek *angelos*, meaning 'divine messenger'. An angel was a messenger of God, hence the name.

Aisling

Aislinn

Vision, dream

Ashling

A name that has been very popular since the nineteenth century. It was used to describe a type of nostalgic poetry, patriotic and romantic, in which Ireland was personified as a beautiful woman, and then became a personal name. Its lovely sound is part of its attraction.

Alannah
Alanna, Alana
Child

A nineteenth-century form of the Gaelic term of endearment, *a leanbh* ('child'), hence its popularity as a first name.

Alva
Almha

In legend, Almha was an Irish goddess, renowned for her strength and prowess. She was one of the Tuatha Dé Danann ('people of Dana'), a mythical tribe of gods said to have been the ancestors of the Irish people. At Almu in Leinster there is a hill and fortress named after her.

Aodhamair
Aedammair, Adamair
Fire

A girl's name derived from the boy's name Áed ('fire'). It was the name of the first woman said to have been 'given the veil' (made a nun) by St Patrick; her father was called Áed. She founded a nunnery at Drom Dubhain, near Clogher, Co. Tyrone (her feast day: 18 January).

Aoibheall
Aíbell
Radiance, spark, fire

The name of one of the old Irish goddesses, which has retained its pagan associations. Some legends say she is a fairy woman who lives in the fairy mound of Craig Liath, near Killaloe, Co. Clare, and that she appeared to the great Irish high king Brian Boru the night before the Battle of Clontarf in 1014. Other legends mention Aíbell, the daughter of the Ulster warrior Celchar mac Uithechair, and Aíbell Grúuadsolus ('Aíbell of the bright cheeks'), the king of Munster's daughter.

Aoife

Aife

Eva

Beautiful, radiant

A name, probably that of a goddess, which was very common among the heroines of early Irish legends. Aoife was the sister of the female warrior Scathach, who instructed Cúchulainn, the great Ulster warrior, in the martial arts. Aoife fell in love with him and had his son. The child became a warrior and was later killed by his father, who did not know he was his son. Aoife, the daughter of Diarmaid, king of Leinster, married Strongbow, the leader of the Norman invaders.

Attracta

Athracht

A name with obvious attractions that was very popular at the turn of the nineteenth century. It was the name of a sixth-century saint from Sligo. She founded a nunnery at Killaraght, Co. Mayo, a settlement named after her.

Báirbre
Strange, savage, uncouth
Barbara

A name derived from the Greek word for 'strange'. St Barbara was one of the church's early saints. It is said that her father was turned to ashes by a bolt of lightning when he tried to have her put to death for refusing to renounce Christianity. She became the patron saint of artillerymen.

Béibhinn
Bébinn, Béfind, Bébhionn   *Fair woman*   *Bevin, Bevan*

A popular name in medieval Ireland, it is derived from *bean* ('woman') and *fionn* ('fair'), and may originally have been used to describe Viking women. The mother and daughter of Brian Boru, the great Irish high king who expelled the Norsemen at the Battle of Clontarf in 1014, both had this name. In Irish mythology, the golden-haired giantess Béibhinn fled from her giant husband Aodh Álainn ('the beautiful') and sought sanctuary with Fionn mac Cumhail, leader of the warrior band the Fianna.

Bernadette
Bearnairdín

An imported name, it is the diminutive of the French form of Bernard. It became very popular after the Virgin Mary was said to have appeared to St Bernadette Soubirous in Lourdes in 1858. She was canonised in 1933.

Bétéide
Bé Téite   *Wanton woman*

In legend, Bétéide was one of the Tuatha Dé Danann, the mythical race said to have been the first inhabitants of Ireland. She was the daughter of Flidais.

Blánaid

Bláthnáit, Bláthnat,
Bláthnaid

Little flower

Blánaid was the wife of Cú Roí, a king of Munster. She fell in love with Cúchulainn, the Ulster warrior and her husband's rival. Cú Roí's fortress was constructed so that no one could find the entrance. Blánaid revealed the secret entrance to Cúchulainn by pouring milk into a stream that flowed through the fortress. Cúchulainn watched where the milk-stained water emerged, entered the fortress and seized it. Cú Roí was killed and Cúchulainn and Blánaid fled. In vengeance, the king's poet seized her and jumped with her to their deaths from the cliff-top of Cenn Bera, on the Beara peninsula on the west coast of Ireland.

Branna

Brannagh

Raven-black

An attractive name taken from the Irish word *bran* ('raven'). It is a way of saying 'beauty with hair as dark as a raven', so it is a perfect name for a black-haired baby girl.

Bree

Exalted one

This could be a form of the name Brigid, or a name in its own right that comes from a similar root. The name suggests spirituality (it means 'exalted one'), and is an element in names currently very popular in the United States, such as Breeanne and Breeanna.

Brianna

Briana, Bryana, Brianne

Noble, virtuous

Very popular in the United States and Canada, this is a modern female form of the Irish boy's name Brian.

Brigid

Bríd, Brighid, Brigit   *High goddess, strength*   *Bridget*

The name of the greatest of the Irish saints, and of the Celtic goddess of agriculture, healing and poetry. The latter's festival, Imbolc (1 February), marked the beginning of the Celtic spring. St Brigid of Kildare was born *c*.450 and established a great convent there. She died *c*.523. The custom of plaiting 'Brigid's crosses', made of rushes or straw, takes place on her feast day, also 1 February. The name was so often given to Irish girls that 'Biddy' was used to mean any Irish girl. Many who went to America as maids were automatically called 'Biddy'.

Bronagh

Brónach   *Sorrowful*   *Dolores*
          (see separate entry)

This was a rare early name in Ireland and at one time was used for girls and boys. Brónach was the patron saint of seafarers. St Brónach's well is found in Kilbroney, Co. Down. The saint's crozier is preserved in Dublin's National Museum and her bell in the Catholic church in Rostrevor. Her feast day: 2 April.

Cairenn
Beloved little one

Caireann   *Karen, Karin*

A name that may be derived from the Gaelic *cara* ('beloved'), with the diminutive -*in*, so meaning 'beloved little one'. It could also be an Irish form of the Latin name Carina. Cairenn Chasdubh ('Cairenn of the dark curly hair') was the daughter of the king of the Saxons, the mistress of King Eochu and mother of the great warrior Niall of the Nine Hostages. She was therefore the maternal ancestor of Ireland's high kings. She was harshly treated by Eochu's wife, so a poet fostered Niall until he could claim his inheritance. When Niall became king, he treated Cairenn with love and reverence.

Caitlín
Pure

Caitilín   *Cathleen, Kathleen (see separate entry)*

The name is derived from the old French form Cateline, probably referring to Catherine of Alexandria, said to have been martyred in the early years of the fourth century. St Catherine was associated with courage and purity. The name was introduced into Ireland by the French-speaking Anglo-Normans. During a famine, the Countess Cathleen offered her soul to the devil in exchange for food for the starving. God refused to let him keep it. In the eighteenth century, one of the terms used for Ireland was Caitlín ni Houlihan, a nostalgic reference to the time of the old Irish aristocracy.

Caoilfhinn
Slender and fair

Caoilainn, Cáelfind, Caoilfhionn   *Keelin, Kalin*

A name derived from the Gaelic words *caol* ('slender') and *fionn* ('fair'), it was borne by several saints. Of one it was said: 'This pious lady quickly won the esteem and affection of her sister nuns by her exactness to every duty, as also by her sweet temper, gentle, confiding disposition and unaffected piety.' Her feast day: 3 February.

Caoimhe
Beauty, grace, gentleness   *Keeva, Keva*

A beautiful name and that of a virgin saint from Killeavy, Co. Down (feast day: 2 November). The name may come directly from *caoimhe* (meaning 'gentleness', 'beauty', 'grace') or may be a feminine form of the male name Caoimhín.

Cara
Caragh, Caera   *Friend*

Cara is the Irish word for 'friend', so no greater recommendation is needed for this name, which may originally have come from Latin. In Italian, *cara* means 'beloved'.

Carmel
Garden

A popular Catholic name in Ireland, it comes from the Hebrew word for 'garden' and is used as a mark of reverence for Our Lady of Mount Carmel. Mount Carmel is a mountain ridge in north-west Israel, which extends from the Samarian hills to the Mediterranean.

Cas
Cass   *Curly-haired*

A name whose derivation is linked to a tribe called the Dal Cais, who lived in Ireland in the early period. It was then a common boy's name and, like so many Irish names, can also be used for a girl. To the modern ear, it now sounds more suitable for a girl. The surname, and now first name, Cassidy *(see page 22)*, comes from the same root.

Casey

In the USA:
Casie, Kacie, Kacey

Vigilant in war

A girl's name increasing in popularity, particularly in the United States, it is derived from the popular early Irish name Cathasach. It has several contemporary forms in the USA. It can also be used as a boy's name.

Cassidy
Curly-haired

This is another example of an Irish surname now being used as a first name. The Cassidys possessed healing powers and were physicians to the Maguires, chieftains in Co. Fermanagh from *c.*1300 to 1600. As word of their skills spread, the Cassidys were employed by other Irish chieftains, particularly in the north.

Catriona

Caitríona, Caitrin

Pure

Catherine

The name became popular after the Crusaders brought home stories about Catherine of Alexandria, a legendary and colourful fourth-century martyr. In Ireland, the name became popular through Norman and English influence and by the fifteenth century it was well established among the Irish aristocracy. St Catherine of Siena, in Italy, also popularised the name.

Ciara

Ciar

Dark, black
(in Italian, bright or clear)

Kiera, Kira, Kyra

A name growing in popularity, mainly because of its beautiful sound. St Ciara of Kilkeary, Co. Tipperary, is said to have put out a fire by the power of her prayers. She established two monasteries, the first and most famous at Kilkeary, and died in 679.
Feast days: 5 January and 16 October.

Cliona

Clíodhna, Clídna, Cleona

The name of a goddess of beauty who lived in the Land of Promise and fell in love with a human being, Ciabhán of the Curling Locks. They fled to Glandore, in Co. Cork, but when they landed a great wave came roaring in and drowned Clíodhna. The wave, one of the three great waves of Ireland, is known as 'Clíodhna's Wave'. In legend, a fairy woman has the name. She is one of the Tuatha Dé Danann, the mythical race of gods said to have first inhabited Ireland. They became the underground 'fairy people', whose fairy mounds are still treated with respect by the superstitious. A Cliona was the fairy patroness of the MacCarthys.

Clodagh

Clóideach, Clóda   *Claudia*

The Clóideach is a tributary of the River Suir, in Co. Waterford, and the name became popular after a Marquis of Waterford chose it for one of his daughters.

Colleen

Cailín, Colene, Coleen
Girl or unmarried woman

This name comes from the Irish *cailín* ('girl') and has become popular all over the world, particularly in the United States. It was used by people of Irish descent there, and in Australia and South Africa. The success of Australian author Colleen McCullough's televised book, *The Thorn Birds*, in the 1980s, increased its popularity.

Damhán, Daimíne   **Daimhín**   *Davina, Davin*
Little deer

A name taken from the Gaelic word *damh* ('deer'). Here, with the diminutive *-in*, it means 'little deer'. This form has also produced the surnames Davine and Davane.

Damhnat   **Damhnait**   *Devnet*
Fawn

St Damhnait founded a convent, Tydavnet ('Damhnait's House'), in Co. Monaghan in the sixth century. Her crozier, kept in Dublin's National Museum, was used for the testing of oaths. If someone lied, their mouth became twisted, branding them a liar. Her feast day: 13 June. It is also said to be the name of an Irish virgin martyred in Gheel, Belgium, who is now the town's patron saint. Feast day there: 15 May.

Danu, Ana, Anu   **Dana**
Abundance, wealth

Dana is a very old name, and that of the Irish goddess of abundance, described as 'the mother of the gods of Ireland' by tenth-century king, bishop and scholar Cormac mac Cuilennán. She was the goddess of the Tuatha Dé Danann ('people of Dana'), a mythical race said to have been the first to live in Ireland, and gives her name to a pair of breast-shaped mountains in Co. Kerry. There is also a Christian saint of the name, St Ana (feast day: 18 January).

Darcy
Darcey, D'Arcy, Darcie
Dark-haired

Both a first name and a surname, the D'Arcy form probably came to Ireland with the Normans: it had a long history in France and meant 'fortress'. In Ireland its use was strengthened by the similarity to the Gaelic adjective *dorcha* ('dark', 'dark-haired'): the Irish surname O Dorchaidhe means 'descendant of the dark one'. It is a name that is therefore especially suitable for a dark-haired child. It is a very popular girl's name in the United States today, but was formerly also used for boys.

Darina
Dáiríne, Daireann
Fruitful, bountiful
Doreen

Dáiríne was the younger daughter of Tuathal Teachthmair, the legendary king of Tara, in Co. Meath; she married Eochaidh, the king of Leinster, when his first wife, her sister, Fithir, was said to have died. Both women died of shame when Dáiríne discovered that Fithir was still alive. As a result, their father went to war with Leinster and exacted tribute for many years afterwards. One of the earliest references in legend to Daireann is about a beautiful young woman who fell in love with Fionn mac Cumhail. She asked to be his only wife for a year, and then to have half his time.

Dechtire
Tenth child

Dechtire was the sister of Conchobhar, the king of Ulster, and the mother of Cúchulainn, the great Ulster warrior. The Irish word *deich* means 'ten', so Dechtire may have been a tenth child. The fairies (*sive*) captured her and turned her into a bird, but sometimes she became a woman again, enabling her to conceive Cúchulainn, whose father was the sun god Lugh.

Deirdre
She who chatters

Deirdriú

Deirdre is the most famous woman in Irish mythology, and a source of fascination to poets and writers. The most beautiful woman of her time, she was bethrothed to Conchobhar mac Nessa, king of the Ulstermen, but loved the young warrior Naoise, the eldest of Usna's three sons (Usna was an Ulster chieftain). They ran away to Scotland with Naoise's brothers, but were tricked into returning to Ireland, where Naoise and his brothers were killed. Deirdre threw herself from a chariot, rather than live with Conchobhar. Her story was celebrated by twentieth-century Irish writers W. B. Yeats and John Millington Synge.

Dervla
Daughter of Fál (Ireland)
or *daughter of a poet*

Dearbháil, Derbáil, Deirbhile

An ancient Irish name, originally two words, which may mean 'daughter of Fál', a legendary name for Ireland, or 'daughter of a poet'. St Deirbhile founded a convent in Fallmore, Co. Mayo, in the sixth century. Of a fourteenth-century bearer of the name, the daughter of Áedh O'Donnell, it was said: 'There was never born a woman of her tribe who surpassed her in goodness.' The fame of contemporary Irish travel writer Dervla Murphy has also popularised the name.

Dervorgilla
Daughter of Forgall

Dearbhorgaill, Dervorguilla

Forgall was a god and this name means 'daughter of Forgall'. In legend, the name belonged to a woman who loved Cúchulainn, Ulster's great warrior. He rejected her, but they settled their differences and became as close as brother and sister. Dervorguilla was also the name of a twelfth-century queen who left her husband for Diarmaid, the king of a neighbouring province. She established a church at Clonmacnoise.

Doireann

Doirind, Dáirinn

Daughter of Finn

Doreen

An ancient Irish name, which may mean 'daughter of Finn'. In Irish legend, Doirind and her two sisters, the daughters of Midhir Yellowmane, were given as wives to the sons of the king of Ireland 'since from wives it is that either fortune or misfortune is derived'. Doirind was also the name of the daughter of Bodh Derg, the son of the Dagda (the 'good god'). She wooed Fionn and gave him a magic potion.

Dolores

Sorrows

A popular Catholic first name in Ireland, it is taken from the Spanish title for the Virgin Mary, Maria de los Dolores ('Mary of the Sorrows').

Donla

Donnfhlaidh, Dúnlaith, Dunflaith

Brown princess

Dunla

A name that has become very popular in recent years. It has a long history of royal usage, but could also mean 'lady of the fortress' (*dun* means 'fortress'). Dúnlaith was the daughter of the Connacht warrior, Regamon. Others with the name were the daughter of Fogartach, who died in 773; the wife of the high king Niall Frassach; and the daughter of Flaithbertach, a cleric and high king of Ireland. He died in 764 and she in 798.

Ealga
Noble

An attractive and unusual name, rarely used now and so ripe
for renewed popularity. It is derived from Innis Ealga ('Noble Isle'),
a poetic name for Ireland, so there could be no better reason for
choosing this name.

Echna
Eachna, Echnach   *Horse, steed*

A name taken from *each* ('horse', 'steed'). In legend, Echna was the
daughter of the king of Connacht. She was reputed to be the cleverest
and most beautiful woman of her time. 'The manner of this lady was
this: she had three perfections; for of the world's wise women she was
one, and he whom she should have counselled had as the result both
affluence and consideration.' Of her clothes it was said: 'A smock of royal
silk she had next to her skin; over that an outer tunic of soft silk and
around her a hooded mantle of crimson fastened on her breast with a
golden brooch.'

Eileen
Eibhlín, Aileen, Aibhílín   *Sunlight, life*   *Evelyn, Ellen, Helen*

A name introduced to Ireland by the Normans as Avelina, Evelina and
Emeline, which soon found an Irish form. It was the name of many
aristocratic women in Norman Ireland, including the wife of Walter de
Burgo, the Earl of Ulster, and the daughter of the Red Earl of Ulster. The
form Eibhlín became very popular: Eibhlín Dubh Ní Chonaill composed
the most beautiful of all Irish laments when her husband died. A love
song, '*Eibhlín a Ruan*', written by seventeenth-century harpist Cearbha
O'Dalaigh to his lover, persuaded her to elope with him on her wedding
day. It is still popular at Irish weddings today.

Eilís

Eibhlís, Eilish *God has sworn* or *God is satisfaction* *Elizabeth*

The name of the mother of John the Baptist first came into Ireland with the Anglo-Normans in its Spanish form, Isabella. It was a common Irish name in the Middle Ages. Eilís nic Diarmada Rua was described by the famous blind harpist Turlough Ó Carolan (1670–1732) as 'outshining the rose in beauty'. She was probably the granddaughter of his patrons, the McDermott Roes of Ballyfarnon, Co. Roscommon.

Einín

Eneen *Little bird*

A contemporary name with an obvious appeal, it has already become established as a popular name. It is derived from *éan* ('bird') with the diminutive *-ín*, hence 'little bird'. Endearments in Ireland, as elsewhere, often took the form of birds.

Eireen

Ireland or *peace*

The derivation of this pretty, contemporary name has been attributed to two sources: it could either be a combination of the word for Ireland, Éire, with the Irish diminutive form '*-een*', or it could be an Irish form of the name Irene, meaning 'peace'. Take your pick.

Ethna

Eithne
Kernel

Edna, Ena

This was the name of the mother of Lugh, god of the sun and of arts and crafts, and was a common name in Irish mythology. Historically, Eithne was the wife of Congalach mac Máelmithidh, a king killed by the Vikings in 955. Eithne of the Tuatha Dé Danann ('people of Dana'), in legend the original inhabitants of Ireland, lost her demon guardian and became a Christian. It was also a popular name for saints and the mothers of saints. Eithne and Fedelma, daughters of King Laoghaire, shared the shortest life of any Irish saints: they were instructed, baptised, ordained and 'sanctified' in one day in 433.

Emer

Eimhear, Eimear

Emer was the daughter of Forgall Manach of Leinster. She was said to possess the 'six gifts of womanhood': beauty, a gentle voice, sweet words, wisdom, chastity – and needlework, and was the wife of the great Ulster warrior Cúchulainn. Her father objected to the match, but Cúchulainn single-handedly stormed his fortress and carried Emer off. She bore Cúchulainn's unfaithfulness until he made love to Fand, wife of the sea god Lir. When Emer confronted them, she realised how much Fand loved him and offered to withdraw. Fand was so touched that she returned to her husband. When Cúchulainn died, Emer spoke lovingly at his graveside.

Erin
Of Eire

Erinn, Eryn, Erina

Erin probably means 'of Eire', and is a form of Éire, the name of the goddess that Ireland was named after. In legend, she was one of the Tuatha Dé Danann ('people of Dana'), the ancient gods and inhabitants of Ireland. It is not surprising, therefore, that this name was so widely used by Irish immigrants to Australia, Canada and the United States.

Étáin
Éadaoin, Eadain   *Jealousy*   *Edwina*

According to Celtic mythology, Étáin was 'the most beautiful woman in all Ireland'. The god Midir fell in love with her and took her home. His jealous wife changed Étáin into a pool of water, a worm and then a fly, to hinder his search for her. The fly was blown about by the wind for twice seven years, until it fell into a glass of wine that was drunk by a woman who wanted a child. She gave birth to a daughter, also called Étáin. After many other travails, Étáin and Midir were reunited. It is also the name of the patron saint of Moylurg (Boyle), Co. Roscommon (feast day: 5 July).

Fainche
Fanchea   *Crow*   *Fanny*

The name of many Irish saints, including St Fanchea of Rossory, Co. Fermanagh, who established a monastery there; her brother was Enda of Aran, the father of Irish monasticism, and she persuaded him to take up the religious life. An early king of Cashel, Óengus mac Natfraich, had been a suitor of hers. She was sure she was destined for the religious life, so she successfully steered him towards her sister Dáiríne. Her feast day: 1 January. Fainche is also the name of the saint of Cluain-caoi, near Cashel. Feast day: 21 January.

Fallon
Faithleann, Fallamhan
Leader

A contemporary name that is gaining in popularity, it comes from the old Irish names Faithleann or Fallamhan. It is also a surname (with a second form, Falloon), but is now used more and more as a first name, for girls and boys. To modern tastes it seems more appropriate for a girl.

Fianna
Warrior

The Fianna were Fionn mac Cumhail's band of warriors. In early Ireland, women had equal rights with men, and though warriors were usually men there is a tradition dating from Roman times of Celtic women fighting alongside men, hence this name for a girl. It could also be a combination of the two names Fiona ('wine') and Anna ('full of grace').

Fidelma
Fedelm, Feidhelm
Constancy

A traditional Gaelic name at least 1,500 years old and given to many saints and Irish mythological figures, it was also the name of many famous women in ancient Ireland. Fedelm Noícrothach ('the nine times beautiful') was a female warrior and the daughter of Conchobhar mac Nessa, king of Ulster. She was married to Cairpre Nia Fer, by whom she had a son, Erc, but she eloped with the Ulster warrior Conall Cearnach. He was the foster brother and cousin of the great Ulster warrior Cúchulainn and avenged the latter's death.

Fíona
Fíne
Wine or *fair, beautiful*

Fíona could have been derived from two possible sources: the Latin *vinum* ('wine'), rendered *fíon* in modern Irish, or *fionn* ('fair', 'white', 'beautiful'). Fíona is often used as a shortened form of Lasairfhíona *(see page 40)*. Fíne was an abbess of Kildare, who died in 805.

Fionnuala
Fionnguala, Fionnghuala   *Fair-shouldered*   *Finola*

In mythology, Fionnuala was the daughter of the sea god Lir. She and her brothers were turned into swans for 900 years by Aoife, their jealous stepmother. One Fionnghuala, with her husband, endowed the monastery of Donegal in 1474, in return for it being the burial place for them and their descendants. Fionnuala, mother of the sixteenth-century rebel chieftain Red Hugh O'Donnell, was considered the driving force behind his career. Nuala, the shortened form of Fionnuala, is very popular. Nola and Noleen are also abbreviated forms.

Fionnúir
Fionnabhair   *White sprite*   *Fennore*

Notable women with this name were the daughter of the legendary queen of Connacht, Maeve, and the daughter of Conchobhar mac Nessa, the high king of Ulster. Its meaning is an obvious attraction.

Gael

Gaedheal   *Gail, Gayle, Gaelle*

A name whose derivation and appeal are obvious, since the Gaels were the Celtic inhabitants of early Ireland and gave Ireland its language, Gaelic. They reached Ireland in about 700 BC, having spread eastwards from Central Europe, north of the Alps. *Gael* or *gaedheal* is sometimes used in Celtic communities as a name for a Gaelic speaker or a person from Ireland.

Geraldine

Gearóidín

A popular name in Ireland, it originated with Lady Elizabeth FitzGerald from Kildare, a descendant of the Norman settlers, who was called 'the fair Geraldine' by a sixteenth-century courtier and poet, Surrey. The name has been popular ever since; in the nineteenth century it was widespread in all English-speaking countries. Ger is often used as a shortened form.

Gormlaith

Gormla   *Illustrious princess*

This was a very popular name in early Ireland, particularly among royalty. Many famous women outlived their first husbands and remarried into other dynasties, including Gormlaith, daughter of the king of Leinster. She was first married to Olaf, the Viking leader of Dublin, and gave birth to a son, Sitric. She then married two high kings: Malachy and later Brian Boru.

Grania

Gráinne

She who inspires terror or *corn goddess*

Grace

The best-known Gráinne was betrothed to the great warrior and founder of the Fianna, Fionn mac Cumhail, but eloped with one of his soldiers, Diarmaid. Fionn pursued them for 16 years, with Diarmaid leaving clues around the 'circuit of Ireland', in each place they spent the night, to suggest that he had not slept with her. Megalithic tombs thoughout the country are therefore known as 'Diarmaid and Gráinne's bed'. Gráinne was eventually reconciled with Fionn.

Granuaile

Granuaile or Gráinne Ní Mháille (anglicised as Grace O'Malley) was a renowned sea captain who led 200 sea raiders from the Galway coast in the sixteenth century. She was twice widowed, twice imprisoned, fought Irish and English enemies, was condemned for piracy and finally pardoned by England's Queen Elizabeth I. She died in 1603. She was celebrated in verse and song, and in James Joyce's novel *Finnegan's Wake*. She is often seen as a poetic symbol for Ireland.

Grian

Greine

Sun, sun goddess

Cnoc Greine, near Pallas Green (Pailis Greine), in Co. Limerick, is reputed to be the seat of Grian, the sun goddess. In legend, she is the daughter of Fionn; Loch Greine, in Co. Clare, is named after her.

Hilde
Battle

Hilda

The name of a saintly Irish abbess (feast day: 18 November), and a name that was also made famous by St Hilda, the abbess of Whitby (614–680).

Iseult

Yseult, Isolt, Isolde

In Arthurian legend, Iseult was the beautiful young Irish princess who was betrothed to the elderly king of Cornwall, Mark. Her mother prepared a love potion for her so she would be happy with the king, but Iseult shared it with his young nephew, Tristan, by mistake, and the two fell in love. Their story is the subject of one of Wagner's greatest operas, *Tristan and Isolde*.

Isibéal
God is my oath

Iseabeal, Sibéal

Isabel, Isabella, Sybil

An Irish name based on Isabel, the Spanish form of Elizabeth, which was the name of John the Baptist's mother. All the European forms of the name come from the Hebrew name Elisheba, which means 'God is my oath'.

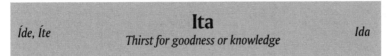

Ita

Íde, Íte *Thirst for goodness or knowledge* *Ida*

St Ita was born in Co. Waterford about 480. She and St Brigid are the
most influential female saints in early Irish Christianity. St Ita, whose
name is said to refer to her hunger for God, was associated with
education and founded an important convent in Kileedy, Co. Limerick.
Kileedy means 'Ita's church'. One of her pupils was said to be St Brendan.
She fasted excessively and is known as the 'foster mother of Irish saints'.
She died at Kileedy in 570; her grave lies at the intersection of the nave
and chancel of the church there. According to legend, she was Jesus's
foster mother. Feast day: 15 January.

Iuchra

In the Finn ballads, Iuchra is the daughter of Ábartach. He turns her rival,
Aífe, into a heron.

Joyce

Seoighe *Lord* *Joy*

This was an Anglo-Norman surname and the name of one of the Galway
tribes. The original derivation was the Breton word for 'lord'. In the past,
the name was used for boys; now it is an exclusively female name.
It is also a surname, known the world over because of the Irish writer
James Joyce.

Kathleen

Caitlín

(see Caitlín) Pure

This is the Irish form of Catherine and has been used so often it has almost become a generic name for Irish girls abroad, for example in the song 'Take Me Home Again, Kathleen'. It came from France in the form Cateline, probably in relation to Catherine of Alexandria, and was introduced into Ireland by the Anglo-Normans. The Irish form is often shortened to Cáit.

Keely

Keeley, Keily, Kiely (also Keela and Kyla)

Beautiful, graceful

A contemporary name that may come from the girl's name Caoilfhionn (usual form Keelin) or may be a feminine form of the boy's name Kiely. In either case the derivation of the name is *cadhla* ('beautiful', 'graceful'), a word found mainly in poetry, so the name implies 'beauty that only poetry can capture'.

Kelly

Ceallach

Red-headed

A name originally used for both girls and boys. Since the mid-twentieth century it has become a very popular girl's name in Britain, the United States, Canada and Australia, and for boys it is again growing in popularity. It was traditionally thought to mean 'church-goer', but more recent opinion holds that it was a much older name meaning 'red-headed'.

Ciarrá

Kerry
Land of the descendants of Ciar

There was no letter 'k' in the Irish Gaelic alphabet. This is a modern Irish name, taken from Co. Kerry, one of Ireland's most beautiful west-coast counties, which means 'land of the descendants of Ciar'. Ciar was the son of the legendary queen Maeve of Connacht. Ciar means 'dark', so the name probably implied someone with dark hair and brown eyes. Kerry is increasing in popularity in Ireland and abroad.

Kyna

A contemporary name with two possible sources: it may come from the Irish word *cion* ('love', 'affection', 'esteem') or from *ciona* ('best', 'champion', 'star').

Laoise
Radiant girl

Laoiseach, Luighseach, Luigsech

Lucy

This name is probably derived from that of the god Lugh, and means 'radiant girl'. The feast day of St Luigsech, or Laoise, is celebrated on 22 May.

Lára
Laurel

Loretta

Laura

The diminutive Loretta is sometimes used because it sounds like Loreto in Italy. Mary and Joseph's house in Nazareth, in which Jesus grew up, was said to have been miraculously transported to Loreto in the thirteenth century. It became the name of a nuns' teaching order: Mother Teresa of Calcutta was trained by the Irish sisters of Loreto.

Lassarina
Flame of the wine

Lasairfhíona, Lasairíona

This is an ancient Irish name, very popular in Connacht in the late Middle Ages, and one regularly given to daughters of the O'Connor family. Fíona is a shortened form of Lasairfhíona. One famous woman with the name Lasairfhíona was the mother of Domnall Beg and 'head of the women of Leth-Cuinn'. She died in 1282.

Líadan Girls' names L *Liban*

Líadan
Líadain
Grey lady

Líadan was a poet whose lover was the poet Cuirithir. On a whim, she rejected him and became a nun. Heartbroken, he became a monk. Both later bitterly regretted their actions. He was exiled and she died on the stone he knelt on to pray. One of her laments exists in a ninth-century manuscript. Another Líadan was the mother of St Ciarán of Seir. Legend has it that while asleep she turned her face to heaven and a star fell into her mouth. In this way she conceived Ciarán.

Liban
Lí Bhan, Lí Ban, Líobhan
Beauty of women

In mythology, Lí Ban (also known as Muirgein), was a half-pagan, half-Christian woman, who lived in Lough Neagh for 300 years. She was eventually caught by a fisherman and became a Christian. In the Ulster tales, Lí Ban is Lúathlám's wife.

Maeve

Meadhbh, Maebh, Méabh

She who intoxicates

The most famous woman with this name was Maeve, the warrior queen of Connacht. She left Conchobhar for her fourth husband, Ailill, and appears in Ireland's greatest epic, *Táin Bó Cuailgne* ('The Cattle Raid of Cooley'), in which she went to war with Ulster to gain Daire's great brown bull. The raid ended in the death of Cúchulainn, the Ulster warrior. The name was also that of the goddess of Tara, in Co. Meath, and wife of the legendary Art mac Cuinn. Maeve also appears as the fairy queen Mab in Shakespeare's *Romeo and Juliet*.

Máire

Máirín

Bitter

Mary

Until the end of the fifteenth century, this name was not given to girls out of reverence for the Virgin Mary. Now it has become a very popular name for girls. The form Muire is used exclusively for the Virgin Mary. In 1532, Máire, the wife of O'Boyle, was thrown from her horse on her own doorstep and died. Máire ní Scolai (1909–85) was well known for collecting, interpreting and performing traditional Irish songs.

Mairéad

Máirghréad, Maighread, Maraid

Pearl

Margaret

This name comes from the Greek *margaron* ('pearl') and has several forms. It was the name of many saints, including St Margaret of Antioch. It was brought to Europe by the Crusaders and introduced into Ireland by the Anglo-Normans, where it has remained very popular, with several forms. St Margaret was also the wife of Malcolm III of Scotland, who died in 1093. He was the son of Duncan; they were portrayed in Shakespeare's *Macbeth*. Mairéad is probably a diminutive of Máire (Mary).

Majella

The Italian surname of St Gerard (1726–55), the patron saint of mothers and childbirth, who was canonised in 1904.

Maolíosa

Máelíosu   *Devotee of Christ*   *Melissa*

A beautiful name most likely derived from *maol* ('devotee', 'follower') and Íosa ('Jesus'), which was initially used by clerics. From the tenth century on, however, its lay usage spread. The best-known bearer of the name was a religious lyric poet who died in 1086. A second possible source could be from the Gaelic word *mil* ('honey'). There are many Irish legends about saints who were beekeepers, so it might have started as a nickname. Originally, it was a boy's name but is now used for girls.

Meara

Sea

A pretty name that probably comes from the Gaelic word *mara* ('sea').

Molly

Mallaidh

A pet name for Mary, which has appeared in Irish songs and stories for over 300 years (e.g. Molly Malone). An Irish form was found for it because it had become so widespread.

Mona
Muadhnait, Muadnat
Noble, good

This attractive name is popular in Ireland and probably used there more often than anywhere else in the world. Several possible derivations have been mooted. It may come from the Gaelic *muadhnait* ('noble'); from the French name Monique ('giver of advice'), introduced by the Normans; or from a shortened form of Madonna ('lady'), as in the Mona Lisa.
St Muadhnait of Drumcliffe, Co. Sligo, was sister to St Molaise, who founded a monastery at Devenish. Her feast day: 6 January.

Mór
Móire
Great one

An ancient Irish name that was the most popular female name in medieval Ireland. The name of a goddess whose descendants became the kings and queens of Munster, it was also a reverential substitute for the name of the Virgin Mary. Mór Mumhan, considered a paragon among Irish women of her time, was the wife of Finghin, king of Munster. She died in 631. Mór, the daughter of Mac Cába, was described as 'the nurse of the learned and destitute of Ireland'. She died in 1527.

Mughain
Young maiden

The name of a goddess and two saints, which comes from the south of Ireland.

Muireann
Mairenn

Sea-white, sea-fair

This is an ancient Irish name. In mythology, Muireann was Oisín's wife. It was also the name of Cael's nurse; he was a Fianna warrior. Muireann composed a poem that won him Credhe, the daughter of the king of Kerry. Another Muireann was the wife of a king of Connacht, Raghallach mac Fuatach, who killed his nephew and was told that he himself would be killed by his own children. Their daughter was brought up by a pious woman and became the fairest woman in Ireland. The king, who did not know she was his daughter, fell in love with her and was beaten to death as a result. Muireann later married the high king, Diarmaid.

Muírgheal
Muirgel

Bright as the sea

Meryl, Muriel, Merrill

A name that was popular in all Celtic regions in the Middle Ages and then fell from favour. It is now becoming popular again. It was the name of a ninth-century wife of the king of Leinster, and of the daughter of the high king Máel Sechnaill I. The latter lived to be very old and died in 926 at Clonmacnoise.

Muirne
Murine

High-spirited

Myrna, Morna

In Irish mythology, Muirne was the mother of the great warrior, Fionn mac Cumhail. She gave birth to him after her husband died, and left him in the care of a female druid and a female warrior.

Nábla

Nápla, Náible　　　　*Lovable*　　　　Annabel

A name with a Latin origin that was brought into Ireland by the Normans, probably in the forms Amabel, Anable and Anaple, all related to the French *aimable* ('lovable', 'beloved'); the initial vowel was lost in the Irish forms.

Naomh
A saint

This is one of several Irish words that have recently been converted into first names. The ancient lists of saints, the martyrologies, were often accused of 'inventing saints out of place names', so there seems to be a precedent for doing so.

Neala

Neila, Neilla, Nelda　　　　*Female champion*

A modern feminine form of the boy's name Niall, it means 'female champion'. It is seen most often in the USA, especially among people whose ancestors came from Northern Ireland, where the allied surnames Neal, Neill, McNeill and O'Neill are commonplace.

Néamhain

Nemon　　　　*Battle fury*

This was the name of an Irish war goddess in ancient times.

46

Nessa
Nease, Neas, Ness
Not gentle

Nessa was Conchobhar's mother. She persuaded her second husband, Fergus, to make Conchobhar king of Ulster for a year, which also increased her own power. Conchobhar ruled so wisely that the people would not allow him to return the kingdom to Fergus. A sister of St Ita also had the name.

Niamh
Niam
Radiance, brightness

The Celtic goddess Niamh Chinn Óir ('Niamh of the Golden Hair') was one of the daughters of the sea god Lir. She seduced Oisín, the warrior Fionn's son, and carried him off on her horse to the Land of Promise. Oisín pined for Ireland, and returned on a magic horse Niamh had provided. She warned him not to dismount, and when he fell off the horse by accident he found that 300 years had passed and he had turned into a blind old man.

Noelle
Nodhlaig, Nollaig
Christmas

The feminine form of Noel, given to a child born at Christmas. The name has only been used in Ireland since the early twentieth century.

Nonín
Daisy

The Irish word for 'daisy', which has only been used as a first name in fairly recent times. Its pretty form and meaning look likely to make it a favourite.

Nora

Nóra *Norah*

Honour

This popular name is the shortened form of Onóra, the Irish form of the Latin Honora, which was introduced into Ireland by the Anglo-Normans. It was quite popular in medieval Ireland, particularly among the O'Briens: three O'Brien daughters had the name between 1579 and 1600. Noreen is a popular diminutive; its Irish form is Nóirín.

Órla

Órlaith, Orfhlaith, Orlagh

Golden princess

One of a series of princesses' names, this was the fourth most popular name in twelfth-century Ireland, when it was the name of a sister and a niece of Brian Boru, the high king. Tiarnán O'Ruairc, king of Breifne, who lost his wife Dervorguilla to Diarmaid mac Murrough, had a daughter called Órlaith. The name fell out of favour in the Middle Ages, but is now very popular again.

Orna

Odharnait, Órnait

Dark-haired

This unusual name is the female form of the boy's name Oran and comes from the word *odhra* ('dark-haired'). It is the name of several saints: one may have established a Christian settlement on Iona before St Columba.

Patricia
Pádraigín, Paidrigín
Noble

The female equivalent of Patrick (Pádraig), Ireland's patron saint, whose
name was derived from the Latin Patricius. There are records of a St
Patricia of Naples, who lived in the seventh century. The name began to
be used in Ireland in the early twentieth century, possibly because it was
the name of one of the granddaughters of Britain's Queen Victoria,
Princess Patricia of Connacht.

Philomena
Powerful friend, loved one

A name with Greek origins, its popularity in Ireland relates to the cult of
St Philomena, whose relics were thought to have been found in Rome in
1802. Their authenticity was subsequently challenged; the Vatican
suppressed her cult in 1960.

Proinnséas
Próinséas, Proinnsias,   *Frances*
Pronsaisín

A popular name in Ireland today, adopted in honour of St Francis of
Assisi (1181–1226), the patron saint of birds and animals. The boy's
name Proinsias, an Irish form of Francis (*see page 102*), was taken from
the Latin Franciscus ('Frenchman'), and this female form has the same
root. It was said that St Francis was given the name because he learned
French so readily. The female form of the name belonged to a saintly
Roman widow: her feast day is 9 March. The earliest examples of the
name in England date from the fifteenth century. It probably passed
from England to Ireland at a later period. The form with '*-ín*' is
sometimes anglicised as Frankie.

Radha
Vision or *red*

The name has become popular in Ireland because of its link with *radharc* ('vision'). It may also be connected with *ruadh* ('red'), so it would be a perfect name for a red-haired girl.

Ranait
Rathnait, Rathnat
Grace, prosperity

St Rathnait is the patron saint of Kilraghts, Co. Antrim (feast day: 5 August).

Realtán
Reailtín   *Star*   *Stella*

The Irish form of Stella, taken from the Latin word for 'star'. Its lovely meaning must recommend it as a girl's name.

Regan
Ríoghán, Rígán
The king's child

A name that can be used for a girl or boy, it comes from the diminutive of *rí* ('king', 'sovereign'). It may also be related to the Irish surname O'Regan, which means 'descendant of a king'.

Ríbh
Stripe

In contemporary rural mythology, Ríbh is associated with a striped cat (the modern Irish word for 'stripe' is *riabh*). If Ríbh lets you stroke the cat, it is said that you'll have good luck.

Ríoghnach
Ríghnach, Ríonach, Ríona
Queenly
Regina

Ríoghnach was the wife of Niall of the Nine Hostages, and mother of
Laeghaire, Énna, Maine, Eoghan, two Conalls and Cairbre. She and her
husband founded a dynasty: it was predicted that 'thine and thy
children's for ever the kingdom and supreme power shall be'. They are
the ancestors of the O'Neills, MacLoughlins, O'Donnells, O'Gallaghers,
O'Gormleys and other northern Irish families. Two of their children, a
Conall and Eoghan, have left their influence in the names of Irish
counties. Ríoghnach is also an Irish saint, the sister of St Finnian of
Clonard (her feast day: 18 December). Another saint with the same name
has her feast day on 9 February.

Ríomthach
Ríofach, Ríomhthach

Ríomthach was the name of one of five sisters who founded a church at
Killiney, Co. Dublin, called Cill Inghean Léinín ('the church of the
daughters of Léníne') in the sixth century. Their brother was St Colman
of Cloyne, Co. Cork.

Ríona
Rionach
Like a queen

A lovely name that comes from *ríon* ('queen'). Mary, the mother of Christ,
is Ríona's special patron, so she has several feast days, including
25 March, 15 August and 8 September.

Róisín
Horse or little rose

Rose

Thought to be derived from the Old German *hros* ('horse'), it has also been connected with the Latin *rosa* ('rose') from earliest times. The name was introduced into Ireland by the Anglo-Normans. Róisín Dubh has been used as a poetic name for Ireland for five centuries. The poet James Clarence Mangan (1803–49) translated a sixteenth-century poem of the same name as 'Dark Rosaleen'. St Rose of Lima was so-called because of the rose-like appearance of her face as a child. Róisín is a diminutive of Róis, which was a popular name for a woman in Ireland long before St Rose was born.

Ruarí
Red-headed ruler

Rori

From *rua* and *rí* ('red-headed ruler'), this is now used as the feminine form of the boy's name Rory.

Ryanne

Derived from *rí* and the diminutive *-in*, meaning 'little king', this name is appearing in the USA as a female form of Ryan.

Saoirse
Freedom, liberty

This is a contemporary example of the adoption of an Irish word as a personal name: it has an obvious appeal. It began to be used in the 1920s (the Irish Free State in the south came into being in 1922) and gained impetus when that became the Republic of Ireland in 1949. It can be used for both boys and girls, but is usually a female name.

Sceanbh
Spike

This unusual name seems to be derived from the Gaelic word *sceanbh* ('spike') and belonged to the wife of a harpist, Craiftine. His harp could either inspire warriors to brave feats or send them to sleep. While her husband was playing, Sceanbh fell in love with Cormac, son of the king of Ulster, Conchobhar.

Seosaimhín
God shall add   *Josephine*

The Irish version of Josephine, this name has French origins. It became popular in France because it was the name of the Emperor Napoleon's wife. It is the feminine form of the Hebrew name Joseph, which means 'God shall add', a name that has been revered in Celtic communities since Christianity was introduced.

Shannon

Shannyn, Channon, Shanyn

The River Shannon is Ireland's longest river, and is probably named after an early Celtic god or goddess. The root of the name is *sen* or *sean* ('old'), so it means 'old one'. It was not often used as a first name in Ireland, but became popular among Irish immigrants to the United States, Canada and Australia in the 1930s. It is still very popular there, and particularly so in Britain.

Shauna
God is gracious

A very popular contemporary name in Ireland at present, it is the feminine form of Sean (the Irish form of John), which means 'God is gracious'.

Sheenagh
God is gracious   *Sheena*

An Irish form of Jane, which itself is a feminine form of John, hence its meaning. It has also been suggested that it could be a form of Sinéad.

Sibéal
Wise woman   *Sybil*

One of the many non-Irish names for which Irish versions were found at the time of the Gaelic revival at the beginning of the twentieth century. It is the Irish equivalent of Isabel, which itself was the Spanish form of Elizabeth.

Síle
Sheila, Sheela, Sheelagh
Pure and musical

A name that comes from the Roman family name Cecilia and was brought to Ireland by the Anglo-Normans. St Cecilia is the patron saint of music. The name may also have been influenced by the Hebrew name Shelah ('longed for'). Síle, the wife of Niall, son of Art O'Neill, was in Omagh Castle in 1471 when it was besieged and captured by Henry O'Neill.

Sinead
Sinéad, Seonaid   *Jane*

This name was introduced into Ireland by the Anglo-Normans as Jehanne, a female form of John. One of the most famous people with this name was Sinéad Flanagan, born in Balbriggan, Co. Dublin, in 1878. A teacher, she taught Irish for the Gaelic League, where one of her pupils was Éamon de Valera, a mathematics teacher and the future president of Ireland. They were married in 1910. She also wrote plays, poems and fairy stories for children.

Siobhan
Siobhán, Sibán   *Lily*   *Joan*

Introduced by the Anglo-Normans and very popular ever since, this was probably a form of the French Jehanne, a feminine form of John. One of Ireland's most famous actresses was Siobhán McKenna (1923–86). She was born in Belfast and moved to Galway with her family when she was five. She acted in the Taibhdhearc, Galway's Irish language theatre, and joined the Abbey Theatre, Dublin, in 1944. She was declared 'Actress of the Year' in 1958. Another notable namesake was Sibán, daughter of the third Earl of Desmond and wife of Tadg mac Carthaig, said to be 'the most celebrated wine-bibber of his age'.

Sive
Sweetness, goodness

Sadb, Sadhbh, Saidhbhe   *Sally*

An ancient Irish name and that of Oisín's mother. She spent part of her life as a fawn because of a spell that had been cast by the Dark Druid, a long-time enemy of the Fianna, the band of warriors. Sadb Sulbair ('of the pleasant speech') was the daughter of Ailill and Maeve, the goddess-queen of Connacht. Other famous women with this name include the wife of the legendary Munster king, Ailill Ólom; Brian Boru's daughter, who died in 1048; and the king of Thomond's wife.

Sorcha
Brightness, light

Sarah, Sally

An old Irish name that was popular in the Middle Ages and remained so until the nineteenth century, when its use declined. It is now becoming popular again in Britain and Ireland.

Súsanna
Lily

This name is the Irish form of the old Hebrew name Susannah. There are also two pet forms: Sósaidh (Susie) and Siú (Sue).

Taillte

Tailltiu

Taillte was the daughter of mac ú Moir in Irish legend and gave her name to Mag Taillten (now Teltown), Co. Meath, where Aonach Taillteann, an ancient assembly, was held at the beginning of August, presided over by the king of Tara. It is a prehistoric cemetery, where games to honour the dead were held. The last assembly was held in 1168, presided over by Ruaidhrí O'Connor. In this way he asserted his claim to the high kingship. The 'Teltown Marriages', thought to be a relic of the old assembly, survived till the eighteenth or nineteenth century. Couples were married in a ring-fort there. If the marriage ran into trouble, they could dissolve it by returning to the fort, standing back to back in the middle, with one then walking south and the other north.

Tallula

Tuilelaith, Tailefhlaith

Abundance of sovereignty, lady of abundance

There were two saints of this name in the eighth and ninth centuries, both abbesses: one of Clonguffin, Co. Meath (died 782); the other of Kildare (died 885; feast day: 6 January). Twilleliah was the anglicised form favoured in the seventeenth century. Tallulah Bankhead, the famous early-twentieth-century American film star, had another form of the name, though in her case it may have come from the Tallulah Falls in Georgia.

Tara

Teamhair, Temair

Eminence, elevated place

In legend, Teamhair is the wife of an early Irish chieftain, but the name also comes from the royal prehistoric site in Teamhair (Tara), Co. Meath. By 500 BC the site had become the central focus of royal and religious power in Ireland, and was the place where the high kings of Ireland were anointed. Temair was the name of the wife of the high king Diarmaid Rúanaid, who died in 665. Through Margaret Mitchell's novel *Gone with the Wind*, and the subsequent film, the name has become internationally popular.

Teagan

Tegan

Beautiful

This unusual name is the Irish form of the Welsh name Tegwen (or Tegwyn), which means 'beautiful', so it needs no further recommendation as a name for a baby girl.

Teffia

Teaffa

An example of a place name, Teffia, in Co. Longford, being used as a first name. It was the name of a woman associated with the site.

Treasa

Treise

Strength

Theresa, Teresa

An old Irish name, this is the Irish form of Theresa or Teresa. It is a very popular name in Ireland because of two inspirational saints: the Carmelite nun St Theresa of Avila (1515–82) and St Theresa of Lisieux (1873–97). There is also a link with the Irish word *treise* ('strength'), which is another reason for the name's popularity.

Tuathla
Princess of the people

A feminine form of the male name Tuathal, its meaning makes it a popular name. Tuathla was a queen of Leinster in the eighth century.

Uaine
Green, verdant

In the Finn legends, Uaine Buide is an enchanting musician, who is accompanied by all the birds in the Land of Promise.

Uallach
Proud

This was the name of the chief poetess of Ireland. She was the daughter of Muimnechán, and died in 934.

Ultana
An Ulsterwoman

A name used mainly in Northern Ireland as a female form of Ultán ('an Ulsterman'). The name was popular in the early period, with 18 saints of the name, including the most famous, St Ultán, the seventh-century abbot, bishop and scholar of Ardbraccan, Co. Meath. He was known for his care of the poor, orphans and the sick and is the patron saint of Ireland's children. A hospital in Dublin is named after him. Another name for the Ardbraccan monastery was Ultán's Well. It was said that St Ultán 'fed with his own hands every child in Erin who had no support', particularly children of women who died of plague. His scholarly works included a poem and a life of St Brigid. His feast day: 4 September.

Una
Úna   *Oonagh, Oona*

In legend, Úna was the mother of Conn of the Hundred Battles. It was a popular name in medieval Ireland. Úna MacDermott is the subject of the seventeenth-century song, 'Úna Bhán' ('Fair Úna'). A poet, Tomás Láidir Costello, fell in love with her. She was much richer than he was and her parents disapproved. Úna started to waste away, but when Tomás visited her she began to recover. He made a promise to wait no longer than half an hour before crossing a stream on the way home, and had just crossed it when he was called back. Because of his vow, he did not return and Úna died. She was buried on an island in Lough Key and he swam out to the island on three successive nights, mourning her in the words of the tragic song.

Boys' names A to Z

Alternative spelling(s)   Name   Anglicised form(s)

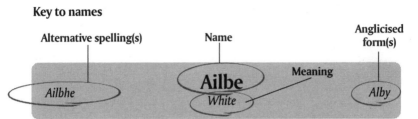

Ailbhe

Ailbe

White   Meaning

Alby

This name is found in both pagan and Christian contexts. St Ailbe of Emly, Co. Tipperary, a bishop of Rome, who died in 527 (feast day: 12 September), helped to bring Christianity to southern Ireland. He was a near contemporary of St Patrick, so was known as 'that other Patrick of the island of Ireland'. Ailbe can also be used as a female name.

Description

Áengus

Oengus, Aonghus, Aongus

One choice, sole strength

Angus

This ancient name was once very common. Five saints are among those with the name, including Óengus Céile Dé (feast day: 11 March), as well as kings, warriors and poets, including Óengus mac Óengusa, the 'chief poet of Ireland', who died in 932. In Celtic mythology, Áengus was the god of youth and love, and the son of Dagda and Boann, after whom the River Boyne was named. He helped lovers, including Diarmaid and Gráinne.

Aidan

Aodhán, Áedán

Little flame

This is a diminutive of Aodh. Several saints had this name, the most famous being Aidan of Lindisfarne, who was sent to convert the Anglo-Saxons in Northumbria, after serving as a monk on Iona. He established a monastery on the island of Lindisfarne, which became the centre for spreading Christianity throughout the north of England.

Ailbe

Ailbhe

White

Alby

This name is found in both pagan and Christian contexts. St Ailbe of Emly, Co. Tipperary, a bishop of Rome, who died in 527 (feast day: 12 September), helped to bring Christianity to southern Ireland. He was a near contemporary of St Patrick, so was known as 'that other Patrick of the island of Ireland'. Ailbe can also be used as a female name.

Ailill
Beauty or rocky place

A name with two possible sources: it may be derived from the Irish word *áilleacht* ('beauty') or from *aileach* ('rocky place'). Ailill was the young husband of Queen Maeve. She chose him, she said, because he was 'a man without meanness, fear or jealousy, a match for my own greatness'. His argument with her over who had the greater herd of cattle led to the Cattle Raid of Cooley, one of the greatest epic tales in Irish mythology. Maeve needed the Brown Bull of Cooley to win the argument, so she went to war to get it.

Aindrias
Andriú　　　*Brave, manly, virile*　　　*Andrew*

The Irish form of the name of the Christian apostle Andrew, the first apostle called by Jesus. The name comes from the Greek Andreas, and has been popular in Celtic communities since the introduction of Christianity.

Alastar
Alusdar, Alusdrann　　*Defender of man*　　*Alastair, Alaisdair*

The Irish form of the Greek name Alexander, the name was introduced into Scotland by Queen Margaret in the twelfth century. Contact between Ireland and Scotland brought it into Northern Ireland, where it became very popular with Irish people of Scots descent.

Alroy
Red

This name would be appropriate for a red-headed boy since it is taken from the Irish word *rua*, which means 'red'.

Aodh
Áed, Aodha, Aoidh   *Fire*   Hugh

An ancient and very common Irish name, this was a favourite among the O'Connors of Connacht and the O'Neills and O'Donnells of Ulster. Hugh O'Neill, the Earl of Tyrone, and Red Hugh O'Donnell, the Earl of Tyrconnell, led a rebellion and defeated the forces of Elizabeth I of England, before being defeated at the Battle of Kinsale in 1601. It is also the name of high kings and many saints, including Áed mac Bricc of Rahugh, Co. Westmeath. His oratory on Slieve League, Co. Donegal, is still a place of pilgrimage on 10 November each year. The abbot of Terryglass, Co. Tipperary, Áed Cruamthainn, compiled *The Book of Leinster* between 1151 and 1224, which is said to 'sum up all the learning of the monastic period of Irish writing'.

Árdal
Ardghal, Ardal   *Great valour, notable warrior*   Arnold

A favourite name in Ulster, most commonly among the MacKenna, MacArdle and MacMahon families, who anglicised it as Arnold. It probably comes from a combination of the words *árd* and *geal* ('high courage').

Ardan
High aspiration

A name taken from the Irish word *ardanach*, which means 'high aspiration'. Ardan was one of the three sons of Usna, an Ulster chieftain. Deirdre had fallen in love with one of his brothers, Naoise, and Ardan helped them escape to Scotland so she would not be forced to marry the king of Ulster, Conchobhar mac Nessa, to whom she was betrothed. They were tricked into returning to Ireland and all three brothers were treacherously murdered.

Art
Bear

An ancient Irish personal name that comes from the old Irish word for 'bear', an animal sacred to the Celts. It is used here in the sense of 'outstanding warrior' or 'champion'. One of the earliest people to bear the name was Art Óenfer (Art the Lonely), a pagan high king, a semi-mythical figure, and father of Cormac mac Airt (Conn of the Hundred Battles). His father's mistress was a demoted goddess called Becuma. She was jealous of Art and sent him on a quest to find a beautiful young woman called Delbchaem. Art rescued her after overcoming many dangers and banished Becuma. Art ruled so honestly that two angels hovered over him in battle.

Barra
Bairrfhionn, Barrfind,   *Fair-haired, fair-headed*   *Barry*
Bairrionn

The name of eight saints, including the patron saint of Cork and Barrfhionn of Kilbarron, Co. Donegal. The latter's voyage to the Land of Promise encouraged St Brendan the Navigator to undertake his great journey. The name was a shortened form of Bartholomew, from the time when biblical names were common. It is a name in its own right, but is often used as a pet form of Finnbarr and Barrfinn.

Bearach

Berach

Spear, javelin hence *pointed, sharp*

Barry

This was a fairly common name in early Ireland and that of several saints, including St Berach, the abbot of Bangor (feast day: 21 April). Another St Berach, who lived in the sixth century, is the patron saint of Kilbarry, Co. Roscommon. He was one of the royal line of Connacht and is the patron saint of the O'Hanlys, who used his name as a family name until the nineteenth century, when they anglicised it as Barry.

Bradan

Salmon

Braden

The Irish word *bradan* means 'salmon'. The Salmon of Knowledge, the Bradan Feasa, appears in Irish legend, and is central to the story of Fionn mac Cumhail, the great warrior of the Fianna, and one of the most important people in Irish mythology. The Fianna was a band of chieftains, warriors, musicians, poets, priests and physicians.

Bran

A raven

This was one of the most popular names in early Ireland and used by the O'Byrnes until after the Middle Ages. In the Finn tales, two warriors in the Fianna have the name. St Bran is the patron saint of Clane, Co. Kildare (feast day: 18 May). Bran Finn, who died in 671, was a famous king and poet, and Bran was also the name of Fionn mac Cumhaill's wolfhound.

Brendan

Breandán, Brénainn,
Bréanainn

Prince

A very popular name, originally said to have come from Wales. It is the
name of many Irish saints, including St Breandán of Birr, but the most
celebrated is Brendan the Navigator (died 577), who undertook a seven-
year journey of discovery. He was said to have been the first European
to reach America. His voyage is the subject of a classic medieval tale,
The Voyage of St Brendan, translated into almost every European
language. Thought to have been born near Tralee, Co. Kerry, he founded
monasteries at Ardfert, Co. Kerry, and Clonfert, Co. Galway.
His feast day: 16 May.

Brennan

Braonán, Braon, Bren

Drop of water or *tear*

Derived from *braon* ('drop of water', hence 'tear'), this name is mostly
used as a surname in Ireland, but is now appearing as a first name in the
United States.

Brian

High, noble

A name thought to be Celtic in origin, and made famous by Ireland's
most celebrated king, Brian Boru. He was acknowledged as Ireland's
high king in 1002 and defeated the Norseman at the Battle of Clontarf in
1014. He united warring dynasties and broke the Viking hold on Ireland,
but died in the battle. In mythology, Brian was the eldest of Tureann's
three sons, the Celtic equivalents of the Greek Argonauts.

Cabhán
Cavan, Kevan, Keevan

This Gaelic name comes from the Irish word *cabhán*, which means 'grassy hill' or 'hollow', but it is usually associated with the name of the Ulster county, Co. Cavan.

Cahal
Cathal
Strong in battle

A popular name in the Middle Ages, borne by kings of Munster and Connacht. In modern times it was popularised by Cathal Brughal (1874–1922), an Irish Republican and politician. Born in Dublin, he joined the Gaelic League and in 1913 became a lieutenant in the Irish Volunteers. He was second in command during the 1916 Easter Rising, and was severely wounded. He served as Minister of Defence between 1919 and 1922, and died of wounds sustained fighting in the civil war.

Canice
Coinneach
Attractive or pleasant person   *Kenneth, Kenny*

The Irish word *coinneach* means 'attractive or pleasant person'. St Coinneach was a sixth-century Irish missionary who founded churches in Ireland, Scotland and Wales. The church he established in Kilkenny, Cill Coinneach ('Coinneach's church'), gave the town its name. It is now renowned as a centre for Irish art and craft.

Carney
Cearnaigh, Cearney, Kearney
Victorious champion

This name is derived from the Gaelic word *cearnach* ('victorious'), which implies 'victorious champion'.

Carrick
Carrig   *A rock*   *Craig*

A name with a straightforward derivation: it is taken from the Irish word *carraig*, which means 'a rock'. It would be a fine name for a boy with a strong, steady character.

Casey
Vigilant in war

Derived from an early Irish name, Cathasach ('vigilant in war'), this name has been used in recent times as a first name in Ireland and the United States. It is used for both boys and girls. It became famous in the twentieth century because of Jonathan Luther 'Casey' Jones (1863–1900), the engine driver on the Cannonball Express in America, who saved his passengers by sacrificing his own life.

Cearbhall
Cearúl, Cearúil   *Fierce warrior*   *Carroll, Carl, Karl*

An ancient name taken directly from the Gaelic word *cearbhall*, which means 'brave in fighting' or 'valorous in battle', hence 'fierce warrior'.

Cian
Ancient, enduring   *Kean*

This was the name of several legendary figures, including Cian, son of the god of medicine. He seduced Ethlínn, the daughter of Balor, who was imprisoned in a tower. Their son was Lugh, the sun god, the father of the Ulster warrior Cúchulainn. It was also the name of the son-in-law of the high king Brian Boru; both were killed at the Battle of Clontarf in 1014.

69

Ciarán
Black

Kieran, Kieron

A very popular name and that of many saints, including Ciarán the Elder, patron saint of Ossory, Co. Offaly. He founded a monastery there, which became the burial place of the kings of Ossory. It is said that a wild boar helped him build his cell by cutting branches with its tusks. (His feast day: 5 March.) The most famous bearer of the name was the abbot of the great monastery of Clonmacnoise, Co. Offaly, which he founded in 547. It became an unrivalled centre of Irish art and literature, retaining its power and influence until the 1550s. (His feast day: 9 September.)

Cillín, Cilléne, Killian

Cillian
Associated with the church
or *good sense*

The name of a famous Irish saint, who was born in Cavan and martyred, with other Irish missionaries, at Wurtzburg in Germany in about 689, by Geilana, the wife of Duke Gozbert. It may come from the word *cill* ('church') and mean 'associated with the church', or from *ciall* ('good sense').

Clancy
Red-headed warrior

An example of a contemporary Irish surname now used as a first name, particularly in the United States. It comes from the Irish words *flann* and *cath*, which mean 'red (-headed) warrior'. The surname came from *mac Fhlannchaidh* ('son of the red warrior').

Clearie

Cleary
Minstrel, scholar

Another example of an Irish surname now being used as a first name, it is derived from the word *cliareach* ('minstrel', 'scholar').

Clooney
Grassy meadow

Cluny

A Gaelic name that has two possible sources: it may be derived from the Irish word *cluain* ('grassy meadow'), or could be connected with an Irish word that sounds similar and means 'flattery'. It is usually a surname, but is now also being used as a first name for boys and girls, a common practice in Ireland.

Cody
Prosperous

A name derived from the surname *mac Óda* ('son of Otto'). Otto was an old German name signifying prosperity. Cody is popular in the United States as a boy's name, but is increasingly also used there as a girl's name.

Coilin
Little chieftain

Colin

A name derived from the Irish word *coll* ('chieftain'), it is used here with the diminutive -*in*, and so means 'little chieftain'. Its meaning is an obvious attraction.

Colman
Little dove

A name with the same root as Colm (*see below*), it means 'little dove' and has developed into a name in its own right. One of hundreds of saints with this name was St Colman of Kilmacduagh, who lived as a recluse until he met the king of Connacht. As the king sat down to dinner on Easter Sunday, the feast was spirited away. The king followed it and found a weakened St Colman devouring it after his Lenten fast.

Colm, Columb
Colum
Dove
Columba

The most famous saint bearing this name is Columcille ('dove of the church'). His guardian angel allowed him to choose his virtues: he chose virginity and wisdom. Because he had chosen the right ones, he was also given the gift of prophecy. He founded several monasteries in Ireland, including, in 546, Doire Cholm Cille, which became modern Londonderry. He then founded the monastery on Iona, in Scotland, where he died in 597. His biography was written by the abbot who succeeded him. His feast day: 9 June.

Connall
Conall
Strong as a wolf or hound
Connell

A name given to early kings and warriors. In legend, Conall Cearnach (Conall the Victorious) was a great warrior who avenged the death of his foster brother Cúchulainn. He was also said to have been Ireland's representative at Christ's crucifixion and one of the people who closed his tomb with a rock and rolled it back on the first Easter Day.

Conn
Wisdom, reason

In mythology, Conn was one of the children of Lir, who were turned into swans by Aoife, their stepmother. The legendary ancestor of the kings of Ireland and many noble Irish families was Conn of the Hundred Battles. He reigned from 177 to 212 and gave his name to the province of Connacht.

Conor
Conchúr, Conchobhar,   *Wolf lover, lover of hounds*   Connor
Conchobar

A name that has been popular in Ireland for centuries. It is taken from the old name Conchobhar and has been shortened and altered with usage. Conchobhar mac Nessa was a legendary king of Ulster. Fergus mac Róich, an exiled hero, said of him: 'This is how Conchobhar spends his time of sovereignty: one third of the day watching the youth, another third playing chess, another third drinking ale till he falls asleep from it. Though we have been exiled by him, I still maintain there is not in Ireland a warrior more wonderful.'

Corey
Corie, Cory, Corry

A name thought to have been derived in Ireland through a variety of surnames that included the root *corra* ('spear'). It may also have been used in Ireland because of its similarity to the Gaelic *cuairteoir* ('visitor'). Ireland has a tradition of hospitality to visitors, known or unknown. It has been popular in the United States as a first name since the 1960s.

Cormac
Charioteer or *son of Corb*

An ancient Irish name borne by kings, saints and warriors, including Cormac mac Airt, one of the legendary high kings of Ireland. The king of Munster, Cormac mac Carthaig, built Cormac's Chapel in Cashel, Co. Tipperary, and was killed in 1138. Cormac mac Cuilennáin was a king, bishop and scholar. He was killed on the battlefield in 908, defeated by the forces of Leinster. His book, *Cormac's Glossary*, is an important work on Irish language, and also contains articles on antiquities, history and mythology. In the seventeenth century, many Irish families changed the name to Charles, after Charles I of England.

Crónán
Cronin, Croney
Dark-skinned, sallow

A name that is probably derived from *crón* ('dark-skinned', 'sallow'). Several saints have this name, but the best-known is St Crónán, who lived in the seventh century and worked with the poor, the homeless and with travellers. He founded a monastery in a remote area of Tipperary, where he was born, but travellers found it hard to find, so he built a new one closer to the roadside. It became the modern town of Roscrea. In north Tipperary, the form Croney is still a traditional name among the O Hogans.

Dáibhí

Dáithí, Daibhead, Dahey   *Swiftness, nimbleness*   *David, Davey*

The Irish form of the biblical name David, the king of the Israelites. Dáithí was the name of the last pagan king of Ireland, who ruled from 405 to 426, and was said to have had 24 sons. With Crimhthan the Great and Niall of the Nine Hostages, he led Irish fleets to raid the Roman Empire. He was killed by lightning in the Alps and is buried under a standing stone called King Dáithí's Stone. There is debate over its location: it is said to be in Co. Roscommon or on the Aran Islands, off the coast of Co. Galway. Another bearer of the name, the bishop of Armagh and papal legate of Ireland, who died in 550, has his name recorded in Latin, as Davidus. The name is also used as a surname.

Dáire

Fruitful, fertile

Dáire is one of the commonest names in Irish legend and mythology, and may have been the name of a god of fertility or a bull god. Donn Cuailgne, the Brown Bull of Cooley, belonged to Dáire mac Fiachna. Dáire's refusal to hand the bull over on a year's loan of 50 heifers to Maeve, the warrior queen of Connacht, was one of the causes of the great battle of Táin Bó Cuailgne between the Ulstermen and the men of Ireland. One saint with the name was a woman (feast day: 8 August), so like many early Irish names, it may have been used by both men and women.

Dálaigh

Dálach   *Counsellor*   *Daley, Daly*

A name that comes from the Irish word *dalach*, which means 'frequenter of gatherings', hence a counsellor or someone who attends meetings. The name also has connections with the word *dáil* ('meeting', 'gathering'). The Irish parliament is called the Dáil. Daley Thompson, the late-twentieth-century Olympic decathlete, helped make the name popular. It is also very common as a surname.

Declan

Deaglán, Declán

Light, gleam

St Declan is the patron saint of Ardmore, Co. Waterford, where he founded a monastery. He is thought to have been one of the earliest Christian missionaries in Ireland, possibly preaching there before St Patrick. He was consecrated by the Pope in Rome, and is said to have met St Patrick on his way back to Ireland. He is reputed to have received a small bell from heaven, which found him a ship and accompanied him on his journey home. It pointed out where he was to build his monastery. An annual pilgrimage is held on his feast day: 24 July.

Dermot

Diarmaid, Diarmait, Diarmuid

Freeman

An ancient name and that of several saints. In Celtic mythology, Diarmaid was the greatest lover in Irish literature. He and Gráinne fled from her husband, Fionn mac Cumhail, who pursued them for 16 years. Historically, it was the name of famous kings: Diarmait mac Cerbaill, the last great pagan king in Ireland, and the high king Diarmait Rúanaid, who died in 665. The high king was king of all Ireland. Diarmaid Mac Murrough, the king of Leinster, brought the Anglo-Normans to Ireland for the first time. He asked them to help him against his enemies.

Derry

Descendant of the red-haired one

A name that comes from the surname O Doireidh, meaning 'descendant of the red-haired one', and increasingly used today as a first name. It is also used as a pet form of Dermot.

Desmond

A popular name in the English-speaking world derived from
Desmumhnach ('man from Desmond'). Desmond was a province in Co.
Cork; its name is derived from *Deas Mumhan* ('south Munster'). The
province was the territory of several powerful dynasties: initially the
MacCarthys, then the FitzGeralds, the Norman settlers.

Dillon

Dylan   *Flash of lightning* or *faithful, loyal*   *Dylan*

This popular name is the Irish form of the Welsh name Dylan and is also
a common surname. It has two possible derivations: it may come from
the Irish word *dealan* ('flash of lightning') or from a word meaning
'faithful', 'loyal'.

Donagh

Donncha, Donnchadh,   *Brown-haired warrior*
Donnchad

This was the name of Brian Boru's eldest son, who became king of
Munster when his father was killed at the Battle of Clontarf in 1014. He
ruled from 1014 to 1064 and died in Rome. The name comes from
donnchadh, which means 'brown-haired warrior'.

Dónal

Domhnall, Domnall　　*World-mighty*　　*Daniel; Donald (in Scotland)*

One of the most ancient and popular Irish names, used throughout the country. Five high kings bore the name, including Domnall Ilchelgach ('of the many treacheries'), who died in 566. In the seventeenth century, Domnall was used as a generic name for an Irish Catholic. In mythology, Domhnall was a Scot who taught Cúchulainn the art of war. The names of the O'Donnell clan from Donegal and the MacDonnells of Antrim and Galloway are derived from this name. One of the few saints with this name is St Domnall. His feast day: 26 April.

Duane

Dwayne, Dwane　　*Descendant of the dark (-haired) one*

A surname now being used as a first name. It comes from O Dubain, meaning 'descendant of the dark (-haired) one'. The name was popularised by the rock guitarist Duane Eddy in the late 1950s and early 1960s and is very popular today in the Caribbean.

Dubhlainn

Black sword　　　　　　*Doolin*

A name derived from the combination of the Gaelic words *dubh* ('black') and *lan* ('blade', 'sword'). Dubhlainn loved the fairy queen and legendary harpist Aoibhell. A prophecy said he was to die in battle, but Aoibhell loved him so much she wove him a cloak that made him invisible.

Dwyer

Dark wisdom

A popular first name, this is an anglicised form of the Irish surname O Duibhidir, which is made up of two elements: *dubh* ('black', 'dark') and *eidir* ('sense', 'wisdom').

Éamon
Rich protection

Éamonn, Éamann   *Edmund, Edward*

The Irish form of Edmond or Edmund, the name was introduced into Ireland by the Anglo-Normans. It was the name of a ninth-century king and saint, martyred in 870, who gave his name to the English town of Bury St Edmunds. One of the most illustrious bearers of the name was Éamon de Valera, one of the great figures in Irish history. He fought in the 1916 Easter Rising, had a central role in the formation of the Republic of Ireland and was Ireland's president from 1959 to 1973. He died in 1975.

Egan
Little flame

Aogán

This is the pet form of Aidan, and is also popular in Ireland as a surname, in this form and as Hagan and O'Hagan. It was the name of a great Irish poet, Aogán Ó Raithaille (1675–1729).

Emmet

Eiméid

Originally a surname and now popular as a first name, it is a tribute to Robert Emmet (1778–1803), who led an unsuccessful rebellion of the United Irishmen against the British in 1798. His love for Sarah Curran led to his capture after an abortive Dublin uprising in 1803. He gave a moving speech from the dock at the scene of his execution in Dublin that same year, which began, 'When my country takes her place among the nations of the earth, then, and not till then, let my epitaph be written.'

Enda
Éanna, Énnae
Birdlike

This was the name of several legendary Irish heroes, including Énnae Airgthech, a king of Munster. It was said he gave his warriors silver shields. The most famous bearer of the name is Énnae of Aran, the Irish monk. Born in Co. Meath, where his father was a chieftain, he was persuaded by his sister, St Fainche, to become a monk. He trained in Galloway in Scotland, and returned to Ireland to establish a monastery on Inishmore, the largest of the Aran islands, off the west coast. He died there *c*.530. His feast day: 21 March.

Ennis
Island or *sole choice*

This name may be derived directly from the Irish word *inis* ('island') or taken from the place name Ennis, a town in Co. Clare that sits on an island between two streams of the River Fergus. Another possibility is that it means 'sole choice'.

Eoghan
Éogan
Born of the yew
Eugene, Owen

A name that often appears in Irish mythology. Eoghan, the son of Durthacht, killed the sons of Usna, an Ulster chieftain, and was driving the chariot from which Deirdre threw herself. Eoghan was also the name of the son of Niall of the Nine Hostages. St Eoghan of Ardstraw, Co. Tyrone, was captured by pirates and taken to Britain. He escaped, studied in Galloway in Scotland and returned to Ireland to found a monastery at Ardstraw. He is the patron saint of Londonderry. His feast day: 23 August.

Eoin

John

A very popular name used in Ireland since the earliest days of Christianity. It is the earliest Irish equivalent of John the apostle's name and came from the Latin Johannes. The later Irish form is Séan, which comes from French, and came into Ireland with the Anglo-Normans. One of the most famous Irishmen bearing the name was Eoin MacNeill. He was a founder of the Gaelic League, chief of staff of the Irish Volunteers, but opposed military action in the 1916 Easter Rising. He became Minister of Education in the first government of the Irish Free State. He was also a scholar, writing on Irish history and Celtic Ireland.

Farrell

Ferrel, Ferrell

Man of strength

An anglicisation of the Irish name Fergal ('man of strength'), this name is widely used as a surname. In the United States, however, it is increasingly seen as a first name.

Ferdia

Ferdiad

Man of God

A name probably derived from *fear* and *Dia* ('man of God'). Ferdia, from Connacht, was a friend of the great Ulster warrior Cúchulainn. When Queen Maeve of Connacht went to war with Ulster, Ferdia had to fight Cúchulainn because the latter was guarding a ford between the two provinces. The duel lasted for three days, and each night the friends tended each other's wounds. Cúchulainn only finally overcame his friend by letting loose his magical spear, the Gae Bolga, which killed Ferdia.

81

Fergal
Fearghal
Man of strength

A name connected with the word *fear* ('man'), it has been popular in Ireland for centuries. It is also the source of the Irish surname Farrell. It is said to be the Irish name of St Virgilius, the non-ordained bishop of Salzburg, who died in 784. Fergal mac Máele Dúin became king of Ireland in 709. He was responsible for murders, for extracting tribute and demanding hostages, and was himself killed at the Hill of Allen in 722.

Fergus
Fearghus
Strength of a man

An ancient Irish name, and one borne by at least ten saints. Fergus mac Róich was an Irish king and an important figure in the great Ulster saga *Táin Bó Cuailgne*. He was tricked out of the kingship of Ulster in favour of Conchobhar and eventually went into exile in Connacht. He was defeated in the ensuing battle against Ulster. In the sixth century, Fergus mac Erc led an army of Irishmen, known as Scoti, to colonise Argyll, thus giving Scotland its modern name.

Fiachra
Raven

In mythology, this was the name of one of the three children of the sea god Lir, who was changed into a swan by his jealous stepmother, Aoife. St Fiachra, who came from Bangor, was the patron saint of travellers, and also of gardeners, because of the fine vegetables he grew around his hermitage at Meaux in France, where he died in 670. He also gave his name to a Parisian horse-drawn cab introduced in the seventeenth century. His feast day: 8 February. Fiacre is the French form of the name.

Finbarr
Fair-haired
Finnbarr, Fionnbharr   *Barry*

A popular name in Ireland today and the name of one of the Tuatha Dé
Danann ('people of Dana'), the mythical race said to have inhabited
Ireland in the earliest times. They became the underground 'fairy
people', and the superstitious still regard their 'fairy mounds' with
respect. Several Irish saints have the name, but the most important is
the seventh-century patron saint of Cork, who is said to have performed
several miraculous cures. He founded a hermitage at Gúgáin Barra
(Barra's Creek), near the source of the River Lee. However, he was told by
angels to follow the river to the position of the present city, where he
founded a monastery. His feast day: 25 September. Barre and Bairre are
Irish 'pet' forms of the name; the latter is anglicised as Barry.

Finn
Fair, light-hued
Fionn

The name of the most important Irish mythological hero, Fionn mac
Cumhail, founder and leader of the Fianna, a warrior band of about 150
chieftains and 4,000 warriors, musicians, poets, priests and physicians.
He acquired the gift of wisdom by touching the Salmon of Knowledge
and sucking his thumb when he burnt it cooking the fish. He was Oisín's
father and pursued Diarmaid and Gráinne. Twentieth-century Irish
writers, such as James Joyce and Flann O'Brien, have used him in their
work as an inspirational figure. In the United States, Finn is becoming a
popular name for girls too.

Finnegan
Fionnagán

A popular diminutive form of Finn.

Finnian

Finian, Finnén

A name derived from the Irish name Finn, with an added British connection: St Finnian of Clonard, Co. Meath, and St Finnian of Movill, Co. Down, both spent time in Britain. It has been suggested that the name might be an early British form of Finbarr.

Fintan

Fionntán

White ancient or white fire

The name of the Salmon of Knowledge, from which Fionn mac Cumhail derived his wisdom, and also the name of one of the sons of Niall of the Nine Hostages. Over 20 saints bear the name, of whom the best-known is St Fintan of Cloneenagh, Co. Laois: he founded a monastery there and is said to have lived on stale barley bread and muddy water. He had a reputation for recruiting disciples in an unorthodox way: it is said he persuaded a man with a wife, 12 sons and seven daughters 'to abandon this world's pleasures and assume the religious habit'. He died in 603. His feast day: 17 February.

Flann

Blood-red

A very popular early name used by kings, queens, poets and saints. Semi-mythological character Flann mac Dima was the lover of the wife of sixth-century high king Diarmaid. The king set fire to a house to try to catch him and Flann drowned in a water tank while trying to escape. Another namesake was Flann Sinna, a high king of Tara, Co. Meath, who died in 916 after reigning 'for 36 years, six months and five days'. He is commemorated on one of the high crosses at Clonmacnoise, Co. Offaly. The name was popularised by the twentieth-century Irish writer Brian O'Nolan, who was known by his pen name, Flann O'Brien.

Flynn
Blood-red

Another example of a surname now used as a first name, it is derived from *flann* ('blood-red').

Gael

According to legend, Gael was the ancestor of the Gaelic people. The name is probably derived from *gaedheal* ('Irish').

Garret
Gearóid, Garalt, Gearalt　　　*Hard as a spear*　　　*Gerald, Gerard*

A name with Germanic origins, introduced by the Anglo-Normans. With the prefix 'Fitz', FitzGerald became the surname of the most powerful Norman-Irish family in late medieval Ireland. Gearóid FitzGerald, the third Earl of Desmond (1338–98) was reputed to have magical powers (it was said he was the product of the rape by his father, Muirís, of the love goddess Áine). He was said to be 'a nobleman of wonderful bounty, cheerfulness in conversation, easy of access, charitable in deeds, a witty and ingenious composer of Irish music' and also wrote courtly love poetry. One tradition says he is not dead, but sleeping in Lough Gur, near his Co. Limerick castle, and will rise up when Ireland is in danger.

85

Garvin
Garbhán, Garbán, Garvan
Rough

The name of five early Irish saints. Little is known about them, but St Garbhán (of Kinsale, Co. Cork or Kinsealy, Co. Dublin), has his feast day on 9 July. It was also the name of an early king of Munster. Like many Irish first names, it can also be used as a surname.

Glendon
Glendan
One from the fortress in the valley

A name that comes from the Gaelic *gleann* (valley) and *dún* (fortress) that together give a meaning of 'one from the fortress in the valley'.

Glenn
Glen
Valley

From the Irish word *gleann* (valley), it is becoming popular as a first name, but is also used as a surname. The Hollywood star Glenn Ford popularised the name in the 1950s. The Welsh form, Glyn, has long been popular.

Iarlaith

Iarlaithe   *Jarlath*

The name of the patron saint of Tuam, Co. Galway, who was ordained in 468 and known for his piety and constant prayer. He established his first monastery and school just west of Tuam, at Cloonfush. Two of his pupils were St Brendan of Clonfert and St Colman of Cloyne. He asked St Brendan to show him a good place to end his days. Brendan took him in a chariot but the wheels broke at Tuam. He founded a second monastery there and died there. His remains are buried on the site of the monastery.

Iollan
One who worships a different god

Iollan was the son of the high king Fergus mac Roth and a champion at the court of Conchobhar mac Nessa. When Deirdre, who was betrothed to King Conchobhar, eloped to Scotland with Naoise, Iollan went with his father to persuade them to come back. He did so, but died defending them when it became clear that Conchobhar's motive had been revenge.

Irial

An unusual and very old Irish name whose origin and meaning are obscure. It was revived by several families in the Middle Ages. Its attractive sound gives it a contemporary appeal.

Kelly
Ceallach
Bright-headed

A name originally used for girls and boys, it is again finding favour for boys. Traditionally, it was thought to mean 'frequenter of churches', but opinion now holds that it is a much older name meaning 'bright-headed'. Since the mid-twentieth century it has become very popular in Britain, the United States, Canada and Australia as a girl's name again. It is also a very common Irish surname.

Kennedy
Cinnéide, Cennétig
Rough-headed or *helmet-headed*

Cennétig mac Lorcain was the father of Brian Boru, Ireland's most famous king, who defeated the Vikings at the Battle of Clontarf in 1014. He united the warring dynasties in Ireland and broke the Viking hold on the country, but died in the battle. In mythology, Brian was the eldest of Tureann's three sons, the Celtic equivalents of the Greek Argonauts. Usually a surname, most famously of America's best-known political dynasty, Kennedy is now increasingly popular as a first name for both boys and girls.

Kevin
Caoimhín, Caoimhghin, Cáemgen
Beautiful birth or *comely child*

The name of a seventh-century abbot, famous for his piety and patience. When he was a young celibate monk he hid in a bed of nettles to escape the attentions of a young woman. The monastery he established at Glendalough, Co. Wicklow, became an important site of pilgrimage, at one stage considered the equivalent of a pilgrimage to Rome. It is said that a blackbird flew on to his hand and laid her egg on it while he was praying one day. He remained kneeling until the egg was hatched and the bird flew away. He died *c*.620. Feast day: 3 June.

Labhrás
Labhras, Lubhrás   *Laurel*   *Laurence*

Several Irish saints had this name, but the best-known was martyred in the third century. Within living memory in Ireland, people associated their suffering with his by saying: 'Labhrás, burned on a gridiron, pray for us.'

Lee
Leigh   *Poem*

This is a popular name for both boys and girls. It may come from the Gaelic word *laoi* ('poem') or be a reference to the River Lee in Ireland.

Lennán
Leannán   *Lover, sweetheart*   *Lennon*

A name that was very popular among the dynastic families of Co. Clare, the Corcu Baiscinn. One of their kings, Lennán mac Cathrannach, ruled from 898 to 915. The modern surname Lennon, for ever associated with John Lennon of the Beatles, who was murdered in 1980, is derived from this name. Because of that association, the name Lennon is now seen as a first name.

Liam

A very popular name that was originally Uilliam, the Irish form of William. It was brought to England at the time of the Norman Conquest, and from there to Ireland. The name William had Germanic origins and was made up of elements meaning 'will' and 'helmet'.

Lochlan
Lochlann, Lochlainn   *Viking*   *Laughlin*

This is the Irish form of a name that meant 'Viking' or 'Scandinavian', since Norway was known as Lochlainn, 'the land of the lochs'. It described the ninth- and tenth-century Viking and merchant invaders. It was given to boys with red or fair hair, and became a common surname in the north-west of Ireland.

Lomán
Lommán   *Bare*

A name taken from the Irish word *lomm* ('bare'). St Lommán, the patron saint of Trim, Co. Meath, is the best-known of the saints with this name. Ancient tradition has it that Fedelmid, the lord of that district, presented 'his territory with all his goods and all of his race' to Lommán and St Patrick. The latter came to Ireland during his reign. Lommán, said to be Patrick's nephew, was the first bishop of the church Patrick founded at Trim and for generations his successors were chosen from Fedelmid's descendants. His feast day: 11 October.

Lonán
Blackbird

A name derived from the word *lon* ('blackbird'). Several saints have the name, including St Lonán Finn (feast day: 22 January) and St Lonán of Trevet, Co. Meath (feast day: 1 November).

Lorcán
Lorccán
Fierce

A very common name in early medieval Ireland and that of several kings. It is now growing in popularity. One of the best-known bearers of the name was the saint Lorcán Ó Tuathail (anglicised as Laurence O'Toole). He studied at the monastery at Glendalough, Co. Wicklow, becoming abbot there in 1153, and became archbishop of Dublin in 1162. He resisted the Anglo-Norman conquest of Ireland, but eventually submitted to the authority of Henry II of England. He died in 1180 in France, and was canonised by Pope Honorius III in 1226.
His feast day: 14 November.

Máirtín

Martán   *Belonging to Mars*   *Martin*

Mars was the Roman god of war and the Irish form of the name was derived from the Latin for his name. It became popular in Ireland because of St Martin of Tours, a fourth-century soldier. It was also the name of the abbot of both Clonmacnoise, Co. Offaly, and Devenish, Co. Roscommon, who died in 868, and the bishop of Roscommon, who died in 915.

Malachy

Maoilseachlainn,
Maeleachlainn,
Malachi   *My messenger*

Originally derived from an old Irish name meaning 'follower of St Sechnall', the name was given to high kings in the ninth and tenth centuries. The modern form became popular in the late Middle Ages and comes from the name of the Old Testament prophet Malachi. It became popular in Ireland because of two saints. The first was the archbishop of Armagh, Maolmaodhog (1094–1148), a papal legate, who reformed the Church in Ireland and brought it closer to Rome and Europe. He was canonised by Pope Clement III in 1190. His feast day: 3 November. The second saint is St Sechnall, one of St Patrick's first converts.

Manus

Mánus, Maghnus   *Great*

A name popular in the north-west of Ireland. It was adopted by the Norsemen in honour of the Holy Roman Emperor, Carolus Magnus (742–814), known as Charlemagne, and introduced by them into Ireland. Charlemagne's court in Aachen was a centre of learning and art; his teachers came mainly from Ireland.

Meallán
Mellán
Lightning

The name of several Irish saints, among them one who was with a group of Irish clerical students said to have met St Patrick. The saint blessed them and gave them a skin to hold their books. The student went on to found a church at Kilrush, Co. Westmeath, and became a bishop, which St Patrick had predicted. His feast day: 28 January.

Mel

The origins of this name are not known but St Mel, the bishop and patron saint of Ardagh, Co. Limerick (died 487; feast day: 6 February), is its most famous bearer. He was St Patrick's nephew and established a monastery at Ardagh. He was reputed – wrongly – to have had a relationship with one of Patrick's sisters, Lupita, who was staying in the monastery. As a result, Patrick issued a decree that 'consecrated men and women – even though nearly related – should live apart, and in separate habitations, lest the weak might be scandalised, or that any injury might be inflicted on religious decorum, by the existence of possible causes leading to temptation.'

Mícheál
Míchél
Who is like the Lord
Michael

This name is taken from one of the biblical Archangels and, like many Irish names, given a Gaelic equivalent. In the nineteenth and twentieth centuries it was very common. One of the most famous modern bearers of the name was the Irish writer and actor Mícheál Mac Liammóir (1899–1978). In 1928 he and Hilton Edwards launched the famous Gate Theatre in Dublin. It brought plays by major European writers to Ireland and provided a platform for plays by Irish writers.

Milo

The Irish names Maeleachlainn, Maolmhuire and Maolmordha, all beginning with *mael/maol* ('devotee of…') were anglicised as Myles and Miles. Milo is an Irish form of these names.

Muiris
Dark-skinned, Moorish
Maurice

This is the Irish form of the name Maurice, introduced into Ireland by the Anglo-Normans and taken from the Latin Mauricius. It was popular because of St Maurice, the Christian captain of a Theban legion, martyred with all his men in Switzerland in the third century by order of Maximinian for refusing to take part in heathen sacrifice.

Murphy
Hound of the sea

Murphy was originally a nickname, then a first name, and later a well-known Irish surname. It is now becoming popular again as a first name for both boys and girls in the United States. It is derived from the Irish word *murchú* ('hound of the sea').

Murtagh
Murchadh
Skilled in seacraft, sea battler
Murdoch (in Scotland)

This was the name of three high kings of Ireland and one of Ireland's greatest military commanders, Murtagh of the Leather Cloak. In midwinter 926, wearing leather cloaks to keep warm, he beat the Vikings in a sea battle on Strangford Lough. He captured and burned Viking Dublin in 939, attacked the Norse settlements in the Scottish islands with an Ulster fleet in 941 and died in combat in 943.

Naoise

Nyce or *Noah*

This name has become popular as a result of the revival of interest in Celtic mythology. In legend, Naoise was the eldest of the three sons of Usna, an Ulster chieftain. Naoise was the lover of Deirdre, who was betrothed to the king of Ulster, Conchobhar mac Nessa. Deirdre said Naoise was exactly the man she wanted, with 'hair the colour of a raven's wing, cheeks the colour of fresh blood, and skin as white as snow'. He fled with her and his brothers to Scotland to escape the king. They were persuaded to return, but all three brothers were treacherously murdered. The name may be associated with the word *nasc* ('bond').

Nevan

Naomhán

Saint, holy one

A name derived from the Irish word *naomb* ('saint', 'holy one') and so originally a nickname for a churchman or a religious person. It was also the name of an Irish saint (feast day: 13 September). It was then used as a first name and later a surname.

Niall

Champion or *passionate, vehement*

Neil, Neill, Neal

An ancient name of uncertain derivation, but increasingly popular. Niall of the Nine Hostages was the semi-mythological king of Tara, in Co. Meath, so the name was given to Irish kings and clan chieftains. It has been suggested that Niall either took hostages from those he defeated in battle or that neighbouring clans gave him a hostage to prove their peaceful intentions. Sithchenn, the smith who lived in Tara, made sure Niall was chosen over his four brothers to succeed his father as king. He lured all the brothers into his forge and set fire to it. Niall brought out the anvil. The surnames MacNeill and O'Neill also come from the name.

Nollaig
Christmas

Noel

This is the Irish word for Christmas, taken from the French form Noël. It has only become popular as a first name in modern times, and can be given to a boy or girl, most often those born on 25 December.

Nuada
Newly made

Nuada was a king of the gods of ancient Ireland, the Tuatha Dé Danann, who lost his hand in battle. Diancecht, the physician of the gods, made him a silver hand so perfect he could pick up a pinch of salt with it. Diancecht's son, Miach, transplanted a hand of flesh and blood on to Nuada's arm.

Nuadu

Nuadha
Cloud-maker

An ancient name associated with a god, possibly the lord of the Otherworld or the god of fishermen. In very early writings, Nuadu is a legendary hero and the ancestor of many noble families: Nuadu Necht, for example, is said to be the legendary ancestor of the Leinstermen. Despite its pagan origins, the name was given to heroes, saints and clerics, including St Nuadu the anchorite (hermit) (feast day: 3 October); and St Nuadu of Clones (feast day: 1 December). It was also the name of the abbot of Tuam and the abbot of Armagh, in the eighth and ninth centuries respectively.

Odhrán

Odrán, Órán, Orin   *Oran*

Dun-coloured, sallow

The name of several saints, the most important of whom was St Patrick's charioteer. St Patrick was on a mission in Munster and a chieftain, Failge Berraide, decided to assassinate him. Odhrán heard of the plot and, pretending to be tired, persuaded St Patrick to change places with him and drive the chariot himself. When they were ambushed, Odhrán was killed. St Oran, the abbot of Meath, was one of 12 people who went with St Columba to the island of Iona to spread Christianity in Scotland: there is a St Oran's well on the island.

Oilibhéar

Oileabhéar   *Oliver*

Relic of God or olive tree

A name derived either from the Norse Olaf ('relic of God') or from the Latin word for 'olive tree', so meaning peace and safety. It was introduced into Ireland by the Anglo-Normans, but became very unpopular in the seventeenth century because of its association with Oliver Cromwell, the scourge of Ireland. It returned to favour because of a saint, Archbishop Oliver Plunkett (1625–81), who was executed at Tyburn in London for treason and canonised in 1976. His head was preserved and kept as a relic in Drogheda, one of the towns where Cromwell carried out an atrocity.

Oisín

Oissíne *Ossian*

Little deer

An old name that is very popular again. Oisín was the son of Fionn mac Cumhail, the most important of Ireland's mythological heroes, who founded and led the Fianna, a band of chieftains, warriors, musicians, poets, priests and physicians. Oisín was the poet of the Fianna and a warrior. It is said that his goddess mother Sive reared him in the forest because she had been turned into a doe. Fionn found him and claimed him as his son. Oisín was also the lover of Niamh, with whom he spent 300 years in Tír-na-n-Óg (the Land of Eternal Youth). It is also the name of four Irish saints.

Oscar

Osgar

Deer lover

In legend, Oscar was the son of Oisín, the great warrior of the Fianna, and so the grandson of Fionn mac Cumhail. In time, Oscar himself became the most celebrated warrior of his day. The Irish writer Oscar Wilde (1854–1900) was the most famous bearer of the name, which fell from favour after the scandal surrounding Wilde's trial. It is now regaining popularity, and has always been used in America. Napoleon Bonaparte, the emperor of France, was so impressed by a poem about Oscar, written by the Scottish poet James Macpherson, that he gave his grandson the name: the child became Oscar I of Sweden.

Patrick

Pádraig, Pádraic, Pátraic

Noble

The name of Ireland's national saint and the quintessential Irish name. It has, however, been popular as a first name for less than 300 years. St Patrick was so revered that his name was not given to children for hundreds of years after his death, except in the form Gilla Pátraic ('servant of Patrick'). There are many legends and traditions about St Patrick (feast day: 17 March), but he was probably born in Britain, captured as a youth by Irish raiders, escaped and trained as a priest in Europe. He made his way back to Ireland and established Christianity as the country's national religion. From 432, he established churches throughout Ireland, over 60 with bishops, the majority of whom were Irishmen consecrated by him. He is said to have performed many miracles and fasted for 40 days on Croagh Patrick, in Co. Mayo. He died in 463. The name Patrick was popular among the Anglo-Normans before it was used by the Irish, who found Irish forms.

Peadar

Peadair

Rock

Peter

The Irish form of Peter, the name of the chief apostle of Christ. The name continues to be very popular because of its provenance. Peadar is a comparatively recent form. Originally the form Piaras was used, which came from Piers, introduced into Ireland by the Normans.

Pearse

Piaras   *Pearce, Pierce, Piers*

This name is also a form of Peter (Piaras was taken from the Norman Piers), and was so popular that it was also adopted as a surname. This is the case with Patrick J. Pearse (1879–1916), the leader of the 1916 Easter Rising in Dublin. The connection with him is one of the main reasons for the name's continuing popularity in Ireland.

Phelan
Wolf

Faolán, Felan

A name taken from a literary word, *faol* ('wolf'). The earliest record of its use appears to be for a follower of the legendary warrior Fionn mac Cumhail. He was so loyal that nothing on earth or in heaven could keep him from his lord.

Phelim
Constant

Feidhlim, Feidhlimid, Felim

An ancient name that occurs in legend and in early royal records: three kings of Munster bore the name. Warriors and poets have also been given the name. Felim was the father of Deirdre, who was the lover of Naoise and was betrothed to the king of Ulster, Conchobhar mac Nessa. It was also the name of Colum Cille's father, so it is most commonly found in Donegal.

Piaras

Perais, Ferus

This name exists in its own right, borrowed from Piers, the Norman form of the biblical name Peter. Those of Norman descent were still using it in Ireland in the seventeenth century. Piaras Feiritéir fought on the side of the indigenous Irish in the rising of 1641, the last of the Kerry commanders to submit to Oliver Cromwell. He seized Tralee Castle, but was wounded in the attack. He was promised safe conduct but was hanged on Martyrs' Hill, Killarney, in 1653, with a priest and a bishop. He was also a scholar and poet, known for his courtly love poems.

Pilib

Filib   *Lover of horses*   *Philip*

The Anglo-Normans brought this name to Ireland. It is the Irish form of Philip, which was itself taken from the Greek. It was the name of one of Christ's 12 apostles and is a very appropriate name for an Irish boy, since the Irish are born with a love of horses in their blood.

Pól

Póil   *Little one*   *Paul*

The Irish version of Paul, which was taken from the Latin *paulus* ('small'). It is, of course, the name of the biblical St Paul, but only became popular in Ireland when Paul VI became Pope in 1963 (he died in 1978).

Proinsias

Proinnsias, Proinnséas,
Próinsias

Frenchman

Francis

This name is an Irish form of Francis, taken from the Latin Franciscus ('Frenchman') and borrowed from St Francis of Assisi (1181–1226), the patron saint of birds and animals. It is said that St Francis was given the name when he was a young man because he learnt to speak French so readily. The name was popularised in Ireland by the Franciscan order of monks.

Quinlan

Quinlevan, Quinlivan,
Quilan

Of beautiful shape

Another example of a contemporary surname now being used as a first name. It is probably derived from *caoindealbhán* ('of beautiful shape').

Quinn

Quin

Intelligent

This name is probably a variant of the name Conn, meaning 'intelligent'. It is the most common surname in Co. Tyrone in Northern Ireland, and is now being used increasingly as a first name, particularly in the USA, for both boys and girls.

Randal

*Raghnall, Ragnall,
Ranulf*　　*Mighty power* or *ruler's advice*

A name that came from the Old Norse name Ragnvald ('ruler's advice')
and was borne by many Vikings who settled in Ireland. It was popular by
the eleventh century: Raghnall mac Amláib was a Norseman killed at the
Battle of Tara, Co. Meath, in 980; Raghnall mac Ímair, the king of
Waterford, died in 1018.

Redmond

*Réamonn, Réamann,
Rémann*　　*Protector, counsellor*　　*Raymond*

The name is an Irish version of an old Germanic name made up of two
elements, *rad* and *mund*, meaning 'counsellor' and 'protector'. It was a
common Norman name and came to Ireland with Strongbow and his
adventurers. It was particularly popular in Northern Ireland. Redmond
O'Hanlon, a notorious seventeenth-century highwayman there, inspired
the verse: 'Twixt Fivemiletown and Crossmaglen, there are more thieves
than honest men.' His father's estate was confiscated by the English
during the Cromwellian settlement and Redmond, his three brothers
and about 50 followers became outlaws. They were known as the
'Rapparees', seeking vengeance on those who had taken Irish lands.

Reilly

Raghallaigh　　*Courageous, valiant*　　*Riley*

Another example of an Irish surname that is now used as a first name,
principally in the USA. It is related to the Gaelic word *rafaireacht*
('prosperity').

Riordan
Ríoghbhardán, Rearden
Royal poet

A name derived from *ri* ('king') and *bardan* ('poet'), it was first used to
describe the profession of royal poet, then became a first name and later
a surname. It is now being used as a first name again, particularly in the
USA and Canada. In an Irish royal household the poet was very highly
esteemed, acting as scholar, historian and adviser to the king.

Risteárd
Strong ruler   *Richard*

A variant of the name Riocárd, introduced into Ireland by the Normans.
Risteárd is now the common form. The name was one of the most
common among the Anglo-Norman settlers in Ireland. Its popularity is
due to a seventh-century Anglo-Saxon king of Kent, who bore the name.
He gave up his throne and became a monk in Lucca, Italy, where he was
said to have performed many miracles.

Ronan
Rónán
Little seal

From the Gaelic word *rón* ('seal'), this is an ancient Irish name. Celtic
legend tells of a seal who is warned not to stray too close to land, but
who is swept ashore by a huge wave and trapped in a human form, as a
'sea maiden'. She lives with a fisherman and their children are known as
'ronans' or 'little seals'. She never loses her longing for the sea, however.
She finds her 'seal skin' hidden by her husband and slips back to the
ocean, but cannot forget her family and can be seen swimming close to
shore, keeping a watchful eye on them. Several saints bear the name.
St Ronan Finn (died 664; feast day: 22 May) put a curse on his tormentor,
Suibhne Gelt ('Mad' Sweeney), who subsequently lost his mind and spent
the rest of his life wandering the woods of Ireland as a wild bird-man.

Rory

Ruaidhrí, Ruairí, Ruarí

Red king or *great king*

A favourite name in medieval Ireland, and that of the last high king, Ruaidhrí Ua Conchobhar (died 1198), who made peace with Henry II of England. It was also the name of a famous sixteenth-century Irish sculptor, Ruaidhrí Ó Tunney, of the Kilkenny school, whose workshop was at nearby Callan.

Rúadhán

Rúadán

Little redhead or *red-haired*

Rowan

This name has been associated with the rowan tree since the time of the Vikings. The rowan is sometimes associated with the tree on which Christ was crucified. In Gaelic mythology, the warrior Rúadhán is the son of Brigit and Bres. It is also the name of several saints, the most famous being St Rúadán, who founded the monastery at Lorrha, Co. Tipperary, in the sixth century (feast day: 15 April). One story says he saved a fugitive from the king by hiding him in his cellar. When the king asked where he was, the saint said, 'I don't know, unless he's under your feet.' Like many Irish saints, he also had the power to cure lepers. When a group arrived at the monastery, he stuck his staff into the ground, water gushed out, and when the lepers bathed in it they were cured.

Ryan

Rían, Ríoghán, Rígán

Little king

The name of saints and warriors, it is mainly a surname in Ireland, but very popular in Britain, the United States and Australia as a first name. Two ninth-century bearers of the name were Rígán, the son of Fergus, who was killed in battle against Connacht in 845, and Rían, son of Bruddai, killed by the Vikings in 895. St Rían's feast day is 23 April.

Seamus

Séamas, Seumas, Seumus   *A supplanter* or *he who takes by the heel*   *James*

A popular name, it is the Irish form of the biblical name James and was common among the Anglo-Norman settlers in Ireland. Notable twentieth-century bearers of the name are the Nobel poet laureate, Seamus Heaney, and Seamus Murphy, a famous Cork sculptor and stone-carver. He was born near Mallow in 1907 and created busts of many prominent people, among them all the Irish presidents. He died in Cork in 1975.

Sean

Séan, Seaghán, Séon   *God is gracious*   *John; also Shaun and Shawn; Shane (in Northern Ireland)*

The Irish form of John, this was one of the commonest names among the early Anglo-Norman settlers in Ireland. Sean is a more recent variation of Eóin. In time Sean became the most popular boy's name in Ireland and was popularised outside the country by the actor Sean Connery. Séan Lemass (1899–1971) was born in Dublin and fought in the 1916 Easter Rising and on the Republican side in the Civil War. He was a founder-member of the political party Fianna Fáil and Minister for Industry in De Valera's first government in 1932. He served as Taoiseach (the prime minister of the Irish Republic) from 1959 to 1966. The phonetic spellings Shaun and Shawn are very popular in Britain and the United States, and Shane in Northern Ireland.

Séathrún

Séafraidh, Séafra, Séafraid   *Geoffrey*

The Irish form of Geoffrey, which was introduced into Ireland by the Anglo-Normans. Irish historian and poet Séathrún Ceitinn (*c.*1570–1650) was born in Co. Tipperary and trained as a priest in an Irish college in Bordeaux, France. He was famous for his sermons and for writing a history of Ireland. He toured the country doing research for the history.

Senan

Seanán, Sionán

Old, i.e. wise

The most famous holder of this name was Seanán of Kilrush, who founded an important island monastery in the sixth century on Inis Cathaig, off the Co. Clare coast in the Shannon estuary. He is said to have got rid of a monster that inhabited the island and arranged with the angel accompanying him that there would always be safe passage for his monks to and from the island. Pebbles from the island are therefore believed to give protection from shipwreck. His feast day: 8 March. The name was first used as a respectful title, then developed into a first name.

Seosamh

Seosap, Seosaph

God shall add (another son)

Joseph

This is now the usual Irish form of the biblical name Joseph. In pre-Norman times, however, the form for the name of the Virgin Mary's carpenter husband was Iósep. He was greatly respected by the early Celtic Church and later became the patron saint of workmen.

Shanley

Venerable warrior

A name that is more usually seen as a surname, but is ripe for popularity as a first name because of its meaning. It is derived from the Irish *sean laoch*, which means 'venerable warrior'.

Sorley

Somhairle

Summer wanderer

An Ulster name that comes from Old Norse and is particularly popular with the MacDonnells of Antrim. In Ireland it became a generic word for Viking, because the Vikings sailed south to raid the coastlines of Ireland and Scotland during the summer, when the weather was better and the journey less hazardous. Somhairle Mac Donnell (1505–90), a thorn in the side of Queen Elizabeth I of England, was imprisoned in Dublin Castle from 1551 to 1552. When he was released, he seized the constable of Carrickfergus and demanded a ransom. He was defeated at Toome in 1575 by Essex. His wife and family, whom he had sent to Rathlin Island for safety, were killed by Sir John Norris, along with the whole of the island's population. Sir Francis Drake was the naval commander in the action.

Suibhne

Suibne

Well-going

Sweeney

The name of seven Irish saints, but the most famous character with this name was Suibhne Gelt ('Mad' Sweeney). Legend has it that he was a seventh-century king of Ireland. He was angered by the incessant ringing of St Ronan's church bells and threw the saint's prayerbook into a lake. St Ronan cursed him and Suibhne is said to have lost his wits. He went to live in the treetops with the birds and flew south in winter. Sweeney has become a contemporary surname.

Tadhg

Tadc　　　　　Poet, philosopher　　　　　*Timothy, Tad (USA)*

An ancient Irish name and that of several kings and princes, including Brian Boru's son, who died in 1023. St Tadhg was martyred at Wurtzburg (his feast day: 8 July). An anglicised form, Teague, was the standard stage name for an Irishman. In modern Irish, Tadhg is used to mean 'the man', as in 'the man in the street' or 'the man in the moon'.

Tiernan

Tiarnán, Tighearnán, Tigernán　　　　　Lord

This was a popular name in early Ireland, given to chieftains, kings and princes. It is usually associated with the surname O'Rourke: the twelfth-century warlike king of Breifne (Cavan, Leitrim and part of Longford) was Tiarnán O'Ruairc. He changed sides so often that by 1152 he had lost his fortress at Dangan and his territorial gains. He lost his wife, Dervorguilla, to Diarmaid Mac Murrough and was assassinated in 1172 by the Anglo-Normans. St Tiernan of Co. Mayo was an early saint (feast day: 8 April). Tiernan is also used as a surname.

Tomás

Twin　　　　　*Thomas*

The Irish form of the biblical name Thomas, one of Christ's disciples. The name was originally used only by the clergy: Tomás, abbot of Linn-Duachail, for example, died in 807. It became popular in Ireland as a first name via the Anglo-Normans, who were devoted to Thomas à Becket, Henry II's Archbishop of Canterbury, murdered in Canterbury Cathedral on the king's orders in 1170. A modern bearer of the name was the author Tomás Ó Criomhthain (1856–1937), who was born and died on Great Blasket island, off the Kerry coast. His book, *The Islandman*, described the hardship and isolation of island life, and was written, he said, because 'there will not be our likes again'.

Torcán
Wild boar

A name derived from the Irish word *torcc* ('wild boar').

Tuathal
Leader or prince of the people   Tully

An ancient name that was given to many Irish kings and heroes, though less common in modern times. It has also been used as a nickname and a surname, but its attractive Gaelic form and meaning suggest it is ripe for popularity again.

Toirdhealbhach,   # Turlough   *Terence*
Tairdelbach,   *Instigator, abettor or shaped like*
Traolach   *Thor (the Norse god of thunder)*

This name became very popular in the Middle Ages: several eleventh- and twelfth-century Irish kings had the name, including Tairdelbach úa Conchobhar, king of Connacht and high king of Ireland, who died in 1156. It was also the name of the famous blind harpist and composer, Turlough O'Carolan (1670–1732), who wrote in Irish Gaelic. He was blinded by smallpox at the age of 14.

Tyrone

Taken from the name of the Irish county, Co. Tyrone, Tir Eoghan ('Land of Eoghan'). The name became popular in the twentieth century through Tyrone Guthrie, the theatre director, and the film actor Tyrone Power. Both men were related through a great-grandfather, who was born in Ireland, in Waterford.

Uinseann
Uinsionn Conquering *Vincent*

The Irish form of Vincent, taken from the Latin Vincentius ('conquering'). The name was introduced into Ireland by the Anglo-Normans, but its popularity is mainly due to the fame of St Vincent de Paul, who founded orders all over the world to care for the poor and sick.

Ultan
Ultán, Ultach Ulsterman

This name was popular in the early period, with 18 saints of the name, including the most famous, St Ultán, the seventh-century abbot, bishop and scholar of Ardbraccan, Co. Meath, who is the patron saint of Ireland's children. He was known for austerity, bathing in cold water whatever the weather: another name for the Ardbraccan monastery was Ultan's Well. St Ultán is said to have 'fed with his own hands every child in Erin who had no support', particularly children of women who died of plague. His scholarly works included a poem and a life of St Brigid.
His feast day: 4 September.

Usna
Temple of the head

In legend, Usna was an Ulster chieftain, and the father of three sons, Naoise, Ainle and Ardan. Naoise fell in love with Deirdre, who was betrothed to the king of Ulster, Conchobhar mac Nessa. She and all three brothers fled, but when they returned to Ireland, all the brothers were treacherously killed by Conchobhar.

Kirby Larson

AUDACITY JONES
STEALS THE
SHOW

* BOOK 2 *

Scholastic Inc.

Copyright © 2017 by Kirby Larson

This book was originally published in hardcover by Scholastic Press in 2017.

ISBN 978-0-545-84066-8

10 9 8 7 6 5 4 3 2 1   18 19 20 21 22

Printed in the U.S.A.   40
First printing 2018

Book design by Carol Ly

For Audrey—who has stolen
Grandma Kirby's heart

"Look at this life—all mystery and magic."
—Harry Houdini

If you, dear reader, have not this very day
observed at least three instances of the magical,
the mysterious, or the miraculous, do set this
book down right away. Find a story
more to your disposition. Perhaps something
about chalk.

CHAPTER ONE

A Somber Ceremony

Audacity Jones peered around the corner, examining the great hallway of Miss Maisie's School for Wayward Girls with utmost care.

"Is the coast clear?" asked someone standing behind her.

"Clear?" echoed the three small voices belonging to the triplets.

Audacity scouted left and right. Not a kid-leather boot nor starched pinafore to be seen in either direction. The dozen other Wayward Girls were no doubt hard at work on the morning lesson.

Thinking of that lesson, Audacity—Audie to her friends—could not help but remember that it was Tuesday. Pastry day. Would that mean éclairs? Brioche? Or the delicacy from Beatrice's hometown, the *canelé*? One of those petite vanilla rum cakes could make the heartiest of souls swoon. Audie sighed. If this was *canelé* day . . . she inhaled sharply, putting an end to such self-indulgent thoughts. There were matters at hand far more significant than creations of pure sweet cream butter, and brown sugar, and—

Audie's confectioned daydream came to an abrupt end with the sudden meeting of an elbow and the delicate space between her ninth and tenth ribs. She turned.

"Sorry, chum." Bimmy's expression was most apologetic. "I didn't mean to bump you."

"No harm done." Audie was instantly forgiving—she needed a reminder to focus upon the task at hand. She checked the hallway once again; still empty.

On tiptoe, Audie led her comrades to their secret spot, a cozy little cubby below the old servants' stairs. Bimmy followed Audie, and three blonde shadows trailed Bimmy. A casual observer might blink thrice in astonishment but, no, said observer would not be hallucinating. On fairy-light feet tripped three petite and identical children, so alike they appeared to be cut out with the same cookie cutter. The first blue-eyed blonde with porcelain skin was Violet, the second Lilac, and the last and smallest (but not the youngest; that was Lilac by four minutes) Lavender.

Bimmy and the triplets were Audie's closest friends at the School for Wayward Girls. Since Bimmy's arrival four years back, the five had been constant companions. As a matter of fact, the quintet had not spent one single day apart until Audie's recent misadventure with the Commodore. Alas, dear reader, there is not sufficient time to further describe those events; I leave it to you to consult a previous volume recounting Audacity Jones's first foray into the rescue business.

Like a pinafored centipede, the five girls moved as one across the worn cabbage roses of the hallway runner. They paced twenty steps south, twelve steps west, and three north until they reached the three-quarter door, nearly hidden from view by an overgrown philodendron. Audie, first to reach it, turned the knob and allowed her friends to enter before closing it with a quiet snick.

They settled themselves in a somber circle. From her starched apron pocket—in addition to many other aspects of their daily life, the Waywards' wardrobes had greatly improved since Beatrice's arrival—Audie withdrew a candle nubbin. From the opposite pocket, she produced a match and a flint. With great care, she placed the candle in the center of the circle. With equal care, she struck the match, whose sulfur fumes caused all the girls to cough. Candle lit, she extinguished the match with her breath.

"It is time," she intoned. She reached her right hand out for Bimmy and her left for Violet. Or it might have been Lavender; it was dark in spite of the guttering candle. "As you know, Cypher will arrive on the morrow. And I will venture away with him."

At this, a tear trickled down Lilac's right cheek. Though she knew her friend to be quite capable, she could not contain her worries. After all, Audie's last outing with Cypher, though exhilarating, had proved treacherous. Lilac sniffled.

"No need to fret." Audie handed Lilac a starched handkerchief. She smiled fondly at the triplets, who had been placed in Miss Maisie's care, and thus in Audie's, as infants.

Audie herself had arrived at Miss Maisie's some five years prior. Unlike the sixteen other girls at the School for Wayward Girls, she was not wayward but orphaned; her guardian uncle could not be bothered to discern the difference. He had merely driven Audie to the town of Swayzee, to the school that he'd seen advertised in the *Indianapolis News*. There he presented Miss Maisie with his niece and a tidy sum before striding off without one backward glance at the waif who'd been under his roof less than a fortnight.

Even at the tender age of six, Audie had been resourceful. In the pockets of her little pink pinafore she had stashed a chunk of cheese and two biscuits against possible hunger. And what foresight! She had scarcely been at the School one hour when she offended Miss Maisie with a request to be shown their schoolbooks. That resulted in her first trip of many to the Punishment Room. And it was through one of the room's narrow leaded glass windows that Miniver squeezed for the first time. The chocolate-striped kitten was delighted to share that bit of cheese, an action that had sealed the bond of friendship between Min and Audie.

At the present moment, Min, no longer a kitten, fitted herself through a gap in the old servants' stairs. She padded on white paws around the perimeter of the girls' circle, sniffing. Reconnaissance complete, she leapt onto Audie's lap.

Audie allowed Min to settle before continuing. "Though Cypher has assured us this assignment will be nothing but run-of-the-mill, Beatrice has advised that I not go alone." Here, Audie omitted a significant detail: Since the recent communication from Cypher, her ear had been buzzing to beat the band. You, dear reader, might imagine a buzzing ear a mere inconvenience. But in Audie's case, it was a warning. That buzzing ear had alerted her many times to potential dangers, including her parents' ill-advised and ill-fated safari in the Dutch East Indies.

Audie smiled at her bosom friend. "And Bimmy has agreed to accompany me."

minister of the UU Fellowship of
since September 2002.

"I hope you find here companio
gious journey, challenge to stimu
and your mind, comfort for you
where you can set your hands to
In our Fellowship, we are bound one to another in a
ance and love. We endeavor to bring out the best in o
are committed to bringing our best out into our neig
mindful of Francis David's observation that "we nee
love alike" (Singing the Living Tradition, reading 566

Let's talk together about our free church tradition. Ar
to bring more love, more justice and more hope to all

**2006 WARE LECTURER - POI
Oliver's fierce independence, bea
all driven by a searching mind, ex

An intense and joyful observer o
Thoreau. Her poems are filled wi
shore birds, water snakes, the pha
lands in the same way that Thorea
to the natural world." Honors OI
Pulitzer Prize (1984), and a Gugg

Natural
Reverence

Bimmy returned the smile, though it did not completely cover her true feelings. She would, of course, be Audie's willing companion no matter the destination. But there seemed to be more to Audie's invitation than met the eye. Bimmy scolded herself for such thoughts; if Audie was holding something in reserve, keeping a secret, there was an impeccable reason for doing so. "It's an honor, of course," she said.

Lilac could restrain herself no longer. A tear dribbled down her left cheek.

"Oh, don't be such a milksop," scolded Violet.

"It's not as if they'll encounter the likes of the Commodore again," soothed Lavender.

Lilac dabbed at her eyes. "But I will miss them so."

That one had acknowledged aloud a truth held in common by all unhinged the older-by-seconds sisters. They began to sniffle as well.

"Now, now." Audie, anticipating such a turn of events—the triplets were exceedingly prone to waterworks—had well provisioned her pockets; she was nothing if not prepared. "It sounds as if we will be gone a week at most." She dispensed two additional handkerchiefs. "And you'll be so occupied with those croissant orders for Sharp's General Store that you won't even notice we're gone."

"No matter how busy we are," snuffled Lavender, "we will always notice when you are g-g-gone." The atmosphere at Miss Maisie's School for Wayward Girls had deflated like a day-old balloon after Audie departed on her previous adventure. And now Bimmy would be gone, to boot.

Audie's expression turned tender. "Just think how sweet our reunion will be in one week's time!"

That thought did provide some comfort and stilled the noisiest of the sniffling.

"Now, to the purpose of this assembly." Audie squeezed the hands in each of hers and those squeezes were passed around the circle.

The flickering candlelight cast shadows over Audie's face. It was not a fearful effect; quite the contrary, it was reassuring. "This very day it is my great pleasure to initiate Lilac, Lavender, and Violet into the Order of Percy." She pulled three small fragments of fabric from her pocket.

Many years previous, these fragments had been attached to Audie's beloved stuffed giraffe. But upon the triplets' arrival at Miss Maisie's, it soon became apparent that Percy was the only thing that would comfort Violet. Without flinching, Audie freely gave her toy to the infant. Over the course of the years, Percy had been loved to bits. All that remained were the two nearly bald ears and a raggedy tail.

"By the powers vested in me as the only orphan at Miss Maisie's, I hereby extend to you this invitation. If you accept, answer 'I do with all my heart.'" Audie paused to allow the triplets a moment. "Do you, Lilac, accept this nomination into the Order of Percy and promise to fulfill all of the responsibilities required of such an honor?"

Lilac swallowed hard. "I do, with all my heart."

Lavender responded in the same manner.

Violet, however, asked, "What are the responsibilities?" Her sisters shushed her, but Bimmy jumped right in. "Why, to do whatever Audie might if she were here."

Violet's face assumed an even more serious expression. "There isn't anyone who can do what Audie does."

"It's not so hard." Audie ducked her head modestly.

"Besides, we'll help," pledged Lilac and Lavender.

With a huge sigh, Violet also answered, "I do, with all my heart."

The girls leaned in toward the candle. Audie started them off in the motto she'd taught them. "Things will always turn out splendid in the end, and if it's not splendid, it's not the end," the five recited.

Audie nodded and Bimmy blew out the candle. In an instant, the little space was dense with dark. Despite this, the five girls remained seated, each reflecting on the upcoming week.

The triplets would do their best to fill Audie's kid-leather boots: They envisioned themselves encouraging the younger Waywards, making Professor Teachtest's lessons as lively as possible, and, in general, keeping things running smoothly at the School because, heaven knows, it was beyond Miss Maisie's capacity to do so.

Bimmy's thoughts turned to the coming train journey. All the way to New York City! She and her parents had performed there once, when they'd joined up with the Barley and Bingham Circus.

Audie's thoughts were more practical in nature. She had been delighted, of course, to hear from Cypher and readily agreed to his request for assistance. She would travel anywhere with a man of such high ideals and astonishing capacity for heroism, despite his somewhat dour disposition. And there was the rub. Though Cypher's good qualities were many, he was not overly fond of children—he considered Audie more colleague than child. And he couldn't abide cats.

"I'm hungry," whispered Lilac.

"Me too," whispered Lavender.

"Do you think there are any *canelés* left?" asked Violet.

Audie followed her friends through the tiny door into the grand hallway, giving herself a stern talking-to along the way. Why did she fret so about presenting her case to Cypher? Hadn't she snatched the President's niece from the evil talons of wicked kidnappers? Convincing Cypher to bring Bimmy and Min along on this present mission should be a snap compared to that!

∗ CHAPTER TWO ∗

Quite the Sticky Proposition

"Absolutely not!" Cypher stood tall and resolute in his dark wool suit.

Audie thought he had looked grander in the Secret Service uniform, but evidently guarding President Taft proved too calm for Cypher's taste. He had recently signed on with the Pinkerton National Detective Agency and was now enlisting Audie's help with his first solo case. "I came to gather up one child. Not two children and a cat." He paced in front of the grand Dutch-tiled fireplace in the room formerly known as the Punishment Room but now known to all the Waywards as the library. Miss Maisie, however, still avoided this gracious space at all costs. How one survives without books and stories is beyond comprehension, but there are evidently persons who do not partake of the written word. I know, dear reader, it causes you to shudder as it does me.

Beatrice entered bearing a silver tray from which emanated a rich and honeyed aroma. *"Bonjour, monsieur.* Tea?" Her pale cheeks were brushed with pink as often happened when she was in Cypher's presence.

His attention was diverted from Audie's outrageous request to the offered sweets. "Is that *baghlava*?"

"But of course!" Beatrice blushed a deeper rose. "After the excitation *grande* in the capital city, and your kindness in driving me to Miss Maisie's, it was only good manners to find a recipe from your native Persia as a way to say *merci*."

The notion that Beatrice would trouble herself in this regard seemed to flummox Cypher completely. He was thrown for such a loop that he added both milk and lemon to his tea. In rather astonishing proportions. And he did not even flinch as he took a sip of the disagreeable combination.

"Won't you try one?" Beatrice offered the glazed, layered pastries, glistening with rose water and finely ground pecans. "I know they will not be as, how you say it, *délicieuse*, as those your mother prepared. But perhaps they will remind you of home, in some small way."

Cypher lifted one of the squares to his mouth and took a tentative bite. He chewed. A sigh escaped his lips. From his expression, it was clear he was no longer standing in the library, but had been transported to his desert homeland, seated on rich carpets among loving family and friends.

"They are *bons*, yes?" Beatrice watched anxiously.

His eyes slowly opened. He cleared his throat. "They are"—he licked a crumb from the corner of his mouth—"quite adequate."

Beatrice clapped her hands. "*Merci, merci.*" She held up the tray, urging him to take another. "Please, enjoyment of your tea while I assist the young *mesdemoiselles* with their packing."

"Do have a seat, Cypher," Audie urged. "We're nearly ready."

He chewed, nodding thoughtfully. Then he sat bolt upright in the chair, coughing pecans all over the Tabriz carpet. "No. No. Not *mesdemoiselles* plural." He reached for his teacup, drank, and coughed even harder. "I am here for Audie. Audie alone."

Beatrice wisely removed herself from the library.

Audie perched primly on the reading chair that had belonged to Miss Maisie's late father, Mr. Witherton. "About that."

She studied her patent-leather footwear, a souvenir from her recent adventure in the nation's capital. She wiggled the toes in her left boot, reassuring herself that the remaining precious gold coin from her parents was still safe and secure, its partner having gone to a good cause in Washington, D.C.

As a general rule, Audie was loath to cloak the truth, but she had regrettably learned that there are times when such a strategy is essential. Cypher did not need to know the true reason Audie was keen on Bimmy's company. "Miss Maisie has been under some scrutiny," she began. "By the county board of . . . board. It seems they found her decision to allow me to go off with the Commodore ill-advised." Audie patted the cushioned arms of the reading chair. "From now on, any Wayward who leaves the School must do so in the company of another Wayward."

Cypher blotted at the front of his dark jacket in an attempt to absorb the tea that had sprayed when he coughed. "You said nothing about this when I first wrote you." His hand froze in mid-blot. "Exactly which board?" he inquired. Had Audie not been so extremely fond of him, she would have been crushed at the suspicious nature of the question.

Audie swung her legs, donning a look of sheer innocence. "Oh, you know they don't really let us in on such details." She shrugged, bringing her shoulders daintily up to her ears. "Being that we are mere children."

"This is blackmail," Cypher sputtered.

"Of course"—Audie's legs paused in their swinging—"I could always remain at home."

Cypher nearly growled, "I will agree to the other girl." He set his cup down with a clink and a rattle. "But no cat." His strong hand sliced through the air like a scimitar. "Not even one as clever as Min. And *that* is my final word."

Audie opened her mouth to protest. But a good trader knows when to stop haggling. "I completely understand your feelings." She selected a small piece of *baghlava* and took an experimental bite. Scrumptious! As was everything Beatrice created.

"If you would only tell me a bit more about what I am to do as your assistant, I would be ever so grateful." Audie slowly studied the library's book-lined shelves, from the tip-top of the coved ceiling to the worn oak floorboards, then indicated a row of titles on the nearest bookshelf. "Shall I bring titles on alchemy or horsemanship or rare Chinese herbs?"

"Suit yourself." Cypher stood abruptly. "I am going to the car. I have some headache powders there of which I am suddenly in need." Not unlike a cranky toddler, Cypher stormed out of the room. Audie couldn't be certain, but he might even have been pouting!

A meowing at the window caught Audie's attention. She nudged the sash up to allow admittance. "And where did you get off to?"

she asked as Min leapt gracefully from windowsill to floor. Audie bent to scratch behind the cat's ears.

"I haven't much time, dear Min." Audie smoothed out the skirt of her pinafore as she straightened up. "What reading material shall I take along this time? A good geography book?"

Nethery's New World Atlas had proved quite helpful on the mission with the Commodore. "But that seems redundant. I already know we are going to New York City." Simply speaking the name of that grand metropolis gave Audie a thrill. "I should continue to work on my mathematics, but I have been quite diligent lately. Might I leave that calculus book behind?" Audie crouched to appeal to her friend. Min answered with a jump to the library table and a second leap, which left the cat perched precariously on a shelf that Audie had not much explored in the past.

"Hmm." She pulled out the slim title shifting under Min's paw. *Sleight of Hand: A Practical Manual of Legerdemain for Amateurs and Others* by Edwin Sachs. "This looks quite interesting." She reflected on the postcard that Cypher had sent, first notifying her of his need for her assistance. The image on the front had been of the world-famous magician Harry Houdini. "Good advice, Min. What else?"

The cat's tail snapped back and forth like a metronome. Then it flicked twice more, tapping two additional titles: *Animal Kingdom, Volume 1* and *Harmsworth Natural History*. Audie quickly skimmed the books before adding them to her pile, noting that both seemed to focus on large animals. The library clock chimed the hour. "Oh, I'd best be scooting along." She shifted the books so she could properly pet the top of Min's head, dreading what she must say.

"I do have some wretched news, stalwart friend. It appears Cypher is quite firm about you remaining behind at the School."

Min meowed.

The disappointment in that meow grieved Audie. "It's no doubt for the best." She resettled the slippery stack. "After all, Beatrice has grown so fond of you. And since she's still settling in, I need you to help her." Audie gazed into Min's golden eyes. "I promise to bring you a treat. Perhaps a new collar that will turn Mr. Schumacher's puss green with envy?"

Min shook herself thoroughly, ending with a sharp twitch at the end of her tail. It troubled Audie to see how cross Min was at this turn of events.

"Do let's part on good terms," Audie pleaded.

Another tail flick. A long pause. And then Min padded close, snaking herself around Audie's legs, purring as if a motorboat engine were lodged in her chest.

"That's the spirit!" Audie gave one last pat. "I must be off." She blew Min a kiss and hurried to complete her packing.

Had she glanced back, she would've seen Min leap to the sill and out the open window. After a graceful landing in the rose bed below, the agile cat shook herself slightly before sauntering along as if the ways of humans were of no consequence in the least. Without even bothering to take cover under the hedge of snowball bushes, she made her way to the very automobile where Cypher awaited.

CHAPTER THREE

Patience Is a Virtue

The dark-haired man rummaged in a leather valise on the front seat of an automobile. This auto was not the color of a robin's egg, as had been the case the last time he'd been at Miss Maisie's, but the color of a crow's feather. The chocolate-striped cat recognized it as a method of transport, all the same. She bathed her right front paw as the man shook a powdery substance into his mouth and then washed it down with water from a sterling silver flask. Had the feline been closer and had she been able to read, she would have seen the engraving on the flask: *To Cypher, with great admiration and appreciation, William H. Taft, President of the United States.*

The cat moved on to her second front paw. She had twice previously exerted her special influence on this man; a third time might be problematic. But there would be no question of being left behind. Ridiculous! Where the girl went, so did she. The faithful feline purred, having satisfactorily completed her toilette, then stretched lazily. To her, challenges were like saucers of cream: meant to be licked.

Much to the cat's dismay, the man slid behind the large wheel, hand resting on the leather valise. She was as clever as they come, but this pose made leaping into that leather valise undetected a virtual impossibility.

It should be noted that the cat was a hunter of astonishing ability. Though she did her best to refrain from molesting the wildlife on the grounds of Miss Maisie's School, as that so upset her beloved girl, the cat considered the birds and mice and voles and whatnot beyond the School's borders fair game. And even a kitten knows that skillful hunting requires an infinite supply of patience.

Hunkering low, the cat now drew on that vast well of patience. Though she did not yet know how she would manage it, she would accompany her friend. She had overheard that the automobile was merely being used to ferry its occupants from the School to the train depot. And the train depot was an easy lope away. The catch was how to slip, undetected, onto the train. The cat's tail thumped the driveway as she considered possibilities.

The wait was finally rewarded by her girl and the girl's friend dashing to the car, each with one hand on a hat, and the other wrapped around the handle of a piece of luggage. Cook and Beatrice followed close behind, lugging a sizable wicker picnic basket between them. The basket was jam-packed with provisions sufficient to sustain the travelers on their journey, including— the cat sniffed—tuna salad sandwiches. How thoughtful. And how thoughtful, too, that the picnic basket, when emptied of its victuals, would be exactly the right size to house a certain cat with choco-late-striped fur.

Satisfied, the persistent puss bounded off to the train station.

CHAPTER FOUR

In the Wee Hours of the Morn

As was his custom, the magician had slept but a few hours. Upon waking—the hands on the mantel clock pointed to twelve and three—he slipped quietly from the room he shared with his wife. Bessie was long accustomed to his restless habits; she didn't stir. Did not even open her eyes. And would not open them until a much more civilized hour. Say, noon.

Snugging the sash of his monogrammed silk dressing gown around his trim middle, he strode down the hall and up the stairs to his library-office in slippered feet; the fox terrier, Bobby, followed fast on his heels. Bobby was a new addition to the household, joining it shortly after the passing of Charlie the Pomeranian. Like Charlie, Bobby was a keen student and quickly took to the proscribed repertoire of tricks (remove thoughts of the lowly "shake" and "speak" from your mind); like his master, Bobby had become an escape artist par excellence. In addition, the little tan-and-black terrier was extraordinarily sensitive to the magician's emotional ups and downs. He nosed at the air as he trotted, as if to sniff out whatever might be troubling his man. Should Bobby find the cause, he would grab hold and shake it as his breed does a rat, putting an end to his master's woes.

A reasonable person might surmise that the magician had awakened fretful about his latest boast. Surely this time the famous Harry Houdini had overpromised. Surely not even *he* could pull off such a feat.

But that is not what had roused Houdini from his warm bed. Vanishing a woman, vanishing an elephant: It was merely a matter of scale. Having accomplished the former, he could certainly accomplish the latter. The magician was supremely confident that this new illusion would live up to the grandiose descriptions in the New York press. Descriptions he himself had provided to reporters; among his other many gifts, the magician was a crackerjack self-promoter.

No, he foresaw not one ounce of difficulty in successfully performing the Vanishing Elephant illusion. And what better place to inaugurate such a feat than at the Hippodrome Theater? Every wall in that space, from the promenades to the auditorium, was adorned with elephant heads crafted of marble, each gold tusk punctuated at the tip with a glowing round orb of light. It was one of the few places in New York City, let alone the country, with room enough to house the actual beasts. As luck would have it, Powers' Elephants were that month performing a run at the Hippodrome. The act comprised four enormous Asian females: Lena, Julie, Roxie, and Jennie. It was the latter, Jennie, the largest of the four, that Houdini had in mind to borrow for his new illusion.

He smiled to think of the picture he would make, five foot six with lifts, standing next to the seven-foot-tall Jennie. Without an ounce of fear, he would face the full house, shouting out, "Laadies and gintlemen!" The audience would hear his every word, even in the cheap seats. (The ability to project his voice was yet another of his gifts.) And what a house: Five thousand seats and each occupied by a man, woman, or child eager to see a pachyderm go *poof.*

The magician reached for a sheaf of paper and a pen from his desk. *Prepare to be amazed as Houdini makes a pachyderm go poof,* he wrote. *There* was a line to spark the imagination. He would add it to the handbill he was having printed. Best increase the print run. Ten thousand was more like it.

Bobby sniffed around the edges of the office, stopping at an enormous red trunk labeled M-I. It was one of many that accompanied the magician on his travels. According to Houdini's own inventory, the trunk contained, among a dozen other items, the following: four Mahatma Plumes, one fishbowl trick, and one skull. Bobby's acute sense of smell ascertained that some backstage assistant had stored an onion bagel under the skull during a recent performance. The lingering aroma caused him to lick his chops. He scampered across the room to nudge at the silk dressing gown pocket where oft could be found treats. At the insistent message from the small, damp, black nose, the magician fumbled in said pocket, conjured up a dog biscuit, and tossed it to Bobby, without any demand for a trick in return.

The man was *that* distracted.

Houdini was not troubled about fulfilling a brash promise to vanish an elephant. He could scarcely eat, he was that thrilled to perform it.

No. What drove him from his warm bed at this ungodly hour was a man. A particular man. A child, really. A scientific prodigy by the name of Theo Quinn. Houdini genuinely regretted ever getting involved with Quinn, though, to be fair, there would be no Vanishing Elephant without him. The rough sketches Quinn had mailed were proof of his intellect. Houdini had seen in an instant that the concept was brilliant and, more important, that it would work.

Houdini could handle the illusion with one arm tied behind his back (he was the master of rope escapes, after all). But handling Quinn had become another matter altogether. The boy was most reclusive; he had turned down three invitations to visit Houdini at his stately home in Harlem. Three! Invitations that hundreds—nay, thousands—would jump at.

Time was running out, and Quinn had yet to deliver the final installment of the plans for the illusion. Plans toward which the magician had pledged a substantial sum. Fifteen hundred dollars, to be exact. Plans that were much needed with the performance less than a week away. Did Quinn think elephant-sized wagons could be built in a day? That Houdini could produce the mirrors required from his top hat? Houdini was completely stymied from moving forward as all the specifications were locked in that stubborn scientist's head!

The magician's stomach knotted as he pondered possible reasons for Quinn's recent evasiveness. Had some competitor—that wretched Brindamour for example—gotten to Quinn, bribing him to reveal all? Quinn might be a prodigy in the world of optics, but he would have no idea about the cutthroat nature of magic and magicians. Anything could happen.

"Blast him!" The magician pounded a fist on the desktop; dog and books alike jumped. Houdini caught an inkwell before it tumbled to the floor. Quinn's secrets about the Vanishing Elephant, fairly bought and soon to be paid for, were *his*. And they must remain that way.

Bobby, being relatively new to the household, was not as accustomed as Bess to Houdini's long periods of reflection punctuated by noisy outbursts. The terrier's soft whimpers did not garner any human attention, so he somersaulted across the thick wool rug in hopes of earning another biscuit. This spectacular trick failed to even register with the magician, who was intensely focused on that upstart, Quinn.

A less-than-civilized thought flitted through Houdini's mind. Perhaps that Pinkerton man coming to keep an eye on Theo Quinn could help. Those Pinkertons likely kept company with the lesser class—snitches and cheats and worse—in order to obtain clues and the like. Surely a Pinkerton operative would have the means and resources to—Houdini couldn't resist a throaty chuckle— permanently *vanish* an annoying young man.

That evil thought dissolved as quickly as it appeared. The particular Pinkerton he'd hired was a true gentleman, quite stately, really, with a grip of iron. As strong as Houdini himself, and some eight inches taller. Houdini recalled staring into the man's eyes to determine if he could be trusted. He'd perceived an integrity there rarely found in others he met, especially fellow performers. And, along with that integrity, he sensed a habit of following the straight and narrow path. Houdini sighed. Of course, there would be no shenanigans with Quinn. Not only would the Pinkerton man not agree to it—of that, the magician was certain—but Houdini himself had no taste for violence. No, there would have to be another scheme to handle that confounded nuisance.

While he puzzled over the Quinn problem, Houdini absentmindedly autographed glossy photographs from the large stack on his desk. It was his favorite image of himself: directly and confidently staring at the camera, while heavy chains snaked over and around his nearly naked and powerful physique. The chains were affixed with padlocks at his neck and elbows and wrists and ankles. "Quite the impressive fellow, wouldn't you say, Bobby?"

Hearing his name, the terrier snuffled awake, hopeful for a treat.

An idea flew at Houdini with a flash as bright as a white dove shooting out of a black top hat. "Why, that's it!" He slapped his thigh, and reached for another sheaf of stationery. Hadn't Queen Alexandra fairly swooned upon the occasion of Houdini's audience with her? And hadn't his mere presence often rendered even the toughest and most cynical of newspaper reporters speechless? If Quinn would not come to Harlem, Houdini would go to him. He smiled to think what effect his very presence would have. The poor lad's legs would be atremble. His brain would fail to give him words. He would fall all over himself to be in such esteemed company. Houdini beamed. Take that, you whippersnapper!

The world-famous magician filled his Montblanc fountain pen. *I shall appear to you this very afternoon, at three p.m.*, he wrote in black ink, underlining the words. With that, he sealed the envelope, which the postman would carry away when he came with the first mail delivery of the day.

Bobby, nose resting on front paws, resigned himself to a dearth of treats for the time being. He curled up at his master's slippered feet as Houdini leaned back in his chair, so pleased with this course of action that he closed his eyes and nodded off. The magician remained in that position until his wife called him to luncheon and, whistling a cheery tune, he padded his way down two flights of stairs to join Bess at the elegant and expensive mahogany dining table.

Bobby followed close behind, hopeful of a tidbit of roast beef or morsel of cheese.

CHAPTER FIVE

Sleight of Hand and Disappearing Seatmates

Audie dropped the coin. Again. "I'll never get the hang of this," she grumbled to Bimmy. "You're so much more clever at these parlor tricks than I." She once again studied the pages of Mr. Sachs's book on sleight of hand.

"Don't be discouraged." Bimmy patted her shoulder. "After all, I've been performing since I was no bigger than a candy apple." She had food on her mind; her midsection rumbled for the third time. It had been a long while since they'd eaten. And Cook and Beatrice had prepared such a lovely hamper of food!

As if on cue, Cypher pushed through one end of the train car, bearing the picnic basket. The jostling of the Pennsylvania Railroad train to and fro on the tracks gave him the appearance of a seasick sailor as he made his way to the seat the girls shared. Audie spied a slim volume tucked in his jacket pocket, but she could not glimpse its title. She was pleased to note they shared a passion for books.

A crumpled man wearing a brown-checked waistcoat and a robust imperial moustache entered from the opposite end of the train car a moment later. Audie paused. Was that a faint buzzing in her left ear? If so, this was nothing to be trifled with, as well she knew. Past incidents had signaled misfortunes, great and small. The small included Miss Maisie's dismissal of the triplets' red bumps as an unfortunate encounter with poison oak. Audie's tingling ear had told her otherwise, prompting a phone call to Dr. Holm, who prescribed a triplet quarantine and oatmeal baths, staving off a chicken pox epidemic at the School for Wayward Girls. The great included Audie's parents pooh-poohing of their devoted daughter's warnings, which, tragically, had resulted in Audie's current orphan status.

Audie concentrated. Was that truly a buzzing or merely residual train noise? Not only was the sound as weak as a cup of Miss Maisie's tea, it seemed rather unlikely to find danger within the confines of the Pennsy train car. For one thing, the railroad had an impressive safety record. For another, her fellow traveling companions seemed as worrisome as a clutch of baby chicks. Bees and bonnets, the only thing she and Bimmy had to worry about at this moment was whether to choose a deviled ham or tuna salad sandwich from the picnic hamper.

The crumpled man took his seat across the aisle from the girls and their guardian. "Nice day," he said, with a doff of the hat. Audie and her colleagues could not know it, but the man carried in his bag an assortment of magic tricks and handbills proclaiming the prowess of the Great Oberon, though the man's given name was Wylie Wurme.

"Yes, it is." Audie ignored Cypher's glare. He had rattled off a series of instructions at the Swayzee station, including no speaking to strangers. But that surely didn't apply to their fellow travelers, did it? "I do hope there's some *baghlava*," she said, attempting to change Cypher's frown to a smile. She would never mention it, but in her opinion, he had consumed the lion's share of Beatrice's delicious home-baked treat.

"I think we should begin with something of more nutritional value." Cypher held up two sandwiches. "Which would you prefer?" he asked, waxed-paper packages held in either hand.

"Tuna, please," Bimmy said.

"Me too," Audie said. "Please," she added, almost as an afterthought. Hunger had taken the edge off her manners.

Cypher reached for the remaining sandwich, deviled ham, his least favorite, without complaint. One of his fellow operatives had told him about a Persian restaurant in New York City. He unwrapped his sandwich, dreaming about what he would order should he be able to locate that slice of heaven. *Ghormeh sabzi. Morgh polou. Pilau*, pilaf! He sighed to think of such dishes, taking a bite of the sandwich. He chewed, then paused.

"Is everything all right?" Audie inquired.

Cypher removed several strands of dark brown hair from his mouth. Not hair, he decided upon closer examination; the offending items were more fur-like. This was not only unpleasant but surprising given that Cook and Beatrice kept an immaculate kitchen.

Still, he was hungry. He carefully examined the remaining portion of bread, meat, and butter. There did not appear to be any additional foreign objects. Once the sandwich was dispatched, he reached for the volume in his pocket. Make what you will of its title, dear reader: *Conversational French*.

"It's a long trip." Audie daintily wiped her mouth. "And we've finished *The Wonderful Wizard of Oz*. We took turns reading it aloud. Bimmy does a smash-up job with voices." She sat back against the hard wooden seat, planning her next comment carefully. Cypher was quite impervious to inquisitiveness. "We are in need of a diversion."

Bimmy nodded in agreement, though she wouldn't have minded rereading Mr. L. Frank Baum's story.

"A diversion?" Cypher tugged at his collar band. He'd known the girls would be a bundle of trouble.

"Yes. That or"—Audie primly placed her hands in her lap, delivering the coup de grâce—"tell us about our mission."

Cypher made a shushing gesture, indicating the man in the brown suit.

Audie gave a quick nod. "I meant, tell us about our mission*ary* parents." She smiled in the direction of their traveling companion. "They're saving souls in Borneo. Might *we* share the Good Word with you?" She folded her hands as if in prayer, nudging Bimmy to follow suit.

The man adjusted his hat and found his feet. "I believe I'll make my way to the dining car." He exited their company with tremendous haste.

Audie grinned at her accomplishment. "Now you can tell all," she said.

Cypher found himself in need of those headache powders again. The girl was much too imaginative. One adventure in the nation's capital and she now fancied herself some kind of crime solver.

"*Mission* is an inaccurate term," he clarified. Though it was a step up from assistant soup maker, the role she'd played in their last outing, Audie was likely to be disappointed by the reason she'd been brought along. He cut a glance at Bimmy, correcting himself. *They'd* been brought along.

Cypher slipped the book back in his pocket and reached for his leather valise, never out of his possession. He undid the latches as he brought it to his lap and then removed three ruby-red orbs.

"What are those?" Audie's question was filled with wonder. She had never seen the like.

"Pomegranates!" Bimmy exclaimed. She might not be as well read as Audie, but her vagabond circus life had presented her with a richer variety of experiences.

"What are pomegranates?" The word felt magical in Audie's mouth.

"Delicious!" Bimmy and Cypher answered in unison.

"Sorry," Bimmy said, as if there was something to be forgiven.

"But you are most correct." Cypher hefted one of the fruits in his hand. Then another, then a third. To Audie's delight, the ruby orbs revolved like a sideways carousel in the air.

"You can juggle!" Bimmy clapped her hands in recognition. "I can, too, a bit."

Cypher nodded without breaking the rhythm of his motions. He did some fancy crossover movements, and Audie was certain the pomegranates would fall. But they remained aloft. It was entrancing.

"Ready?"

Bimmy nodded and held out her hands.

"*Zut!*" Cypher called.

The southpaw Wayward expertly caught first one, then two, then three fruits. Bimmy gingerly rotated them in small concentric airborne arcs. When she bobbled one and they all began to tumble, Cypher deftly captured the fruits before they connected with the floor—one, two, three.

"Brava, young lady." Cypher bowed in Bimmy's direction.

She bobbed her head. "You learn a lot in the circus."

Cypher waved his hands over the pomegranates, as a magician might. "And now for the best part of the trick." A knife was removed from his vest pocket and, with expert motions, the skin was slashed in several places. Cypher turned a leathery portion inside out, revealing shiny seed jewels within.

He offered the fruit to Audie. "Try this."

"What do I do?" she asked.

He showed her how to scrape several rows of the juicy seeds into her mouth.

"Oh, it's like eating an adventure!" Audie said.

Bimmy almost declined her share of fruit out of shyness, but she had tasted pomegranates before. They were too delicious to decline because of social insecurity.

The girls ate, taking great care not to drip on their clothes, after Cypher warned them about the fruit's staining properties.

"Where did you learn to do that?" Audie licked tart juice from her fingers. "The juggling, I mean."

The slightest wisp of a smile briefly haunted Cypher's handsome, ruddy face. He preferred not to reveal much of his past. "The house in which I was raised had many children." As he spoke, a few small faces came to his memory, unbidden. The true danger in recalling his homeland revolved around the reason he had left it for America. He blinked away the faces, wrapping the now-seedless pomegranate skins in the waxed paper from his sandwich. "I think you have a saying here, 'Necessity is the mother of invention.' It was of utmost necessity that I invent what you have called diversions."

"Well, it was marvelous." Audie dispatched one last seed, stuck to her lower lip.

"I'm glad you enjoyed it," Cypher said. "Because it's time for you to learn."

"To juggle?" Audie asked. "There will be fruit rolling all over this train if I try."

From his valise, Cypher produced three silk scarves. "This is how one begins." As he had suspected, Audie proved a quick learner. All that reading had worked wonders with her eye-hand coordination. With Bimmy's help, Audie soon graduated from scarves to bean-bags to small wooden balls.

She was flushed with pride at the end of the lesson. And weary. Audie curled up on the seat, murmuring, "Bees and bonnets, that was good fun but I'm bushed." Bimmy likewise curled up. In a thrice, two girlish heads, one with wild auburn locks, one with soft jet-black curls, leaned against each other in slumber.

Cypher pulled the aforementioned book from his pocket and read lists of conversational phrases to himself: *Bonjour. Comment allez-vous? Quelle heure est-il?* Throughout the night, he alternated his studies with watching over the girls, satisfied that the first elements of his plan were falling neatly into place. *Très bien.*

CHAPTER SIX

Theo Quinn, Scientist

Theo's landlord, Billy Bottle, rapped at the laboratory door. "Man here to see you," he announced. For four or five years now, there'd been a steady stream of visitors to the boardinghouse, ever since Theo's first paper had appeared in the *Proceedings of the Royal Society, Series A.* Generally, the visitors were professor types, all black wool robes and wild white hair and ink stains on their middle fingers. This fellow was no scholar, not dressed like a toff, in that three-button cutaway jacket, the way he was.

"Say I had an appointment," the man suggested when the door did not open right away.

Mr. Bottle rubbed his nose, a remarkably large feature that wobbled this way and that over a scrubby moustache. "What I say won't make no difference to Theo." He patted at his pockets. Where had he left his tobacco and pipe? Sometimes it took Theo as long as an hour to answer a knock. If indeed the knock was answered at all.

Impatient with Mr. Bottle, the magician stepped around the man and faced the firmly closed door. "Theo! This is Harry Houdini."

Harry Houdini! The world-famous magician? Mr. Bottle bobbled the packet of Player's, spilling bits of dried material down his stained shirtfront. What was a fella like him wanting with Theo? The landlord brushed himself off, then filled his pipe without further mishap. He tamped the tobacco with a yellow-stained thumb.

"Theo!" Houdini called again.

A match hissed and the aroma of pipe tobacco stung the magician's nose. He sneezed.

"Could be buried in a book," Mr. Bottle offered, puffing gently. "Theo does love them books. One time didn't come out for a solid week."

"I. Do. Not." Houdini exhaled powerfully through his nose. "Have a week."

Billy Bottle cleared his throat. "Something I could do for you?" he asked. "I'm handy in tight spots."

"What? No, you cannot help me." Harry Houdini pushed through the haze of tobacco smoke and bellowed at the door. "Theo! We had an appointment!" Houdini pulled out his solid-gold pocket watch. "For an hour ago."

Billy Bottle consulted his own pocket watch, not that he cared much about the time. It was more to show Houdini he wasn't the only one with such accouterments.

The magician rapped firmly, then leaned his ear to the wood panel, listening. "I can't hear anything," he reported.

Bottle shrugged, bony shoulders bouncing under a threadbare jacket. He put his pocket watch away. "It's them books." He removed a bit of tobacco from his tongue. "Not a durn thing to be done about it." The man didn't have to be so quick about turning down a genuine offer of help. He might be surprised at the tricks old Billy had up his sleeve. Some of them learnt when he'd traveled the roads, selling snake oil, bamboozling hayseeds, and working the side-shows. Billy Bottle knew a thing or two about many of the magical arts.

Houdini massaged the bridge of his nose. "There was money exchanged," he informed the landlord.

"For one of them experiments?" Billy asked, incredulous. None of those professor sorts ever offered a penny for the contraptions and models and thingamabobs Theo created.

"Not an experiment." Houdini was breathing hard. "Furthermore, it is not any of your concern."

Those words made Billy's teeth clamp against his pipe. It was always the same with these big shots. Thought they were too good for the likes of Billy Bottle. "Theo don't much care about money. Says knowledge is all the treasure one needs." Personally, Mr. Bottle would have preferred Theo care a bit more about finances, especially in regard to paying one's rent in a timely manner.

Houdini's face turned as red as the carnation in his lapel. "I am not interested in Theo's life philosophy!" His hand formed a fist and battered the door with enough force to rattle it in its hinges. "This is Harry Houdini. Open up!"

Mr. Bottle puffed serenely. "Theo gets skittery at loud noises."

Harry Houdini stamped his well-buffed oxford—rich brown with cream-colored spats—putting Mr. Bottle in mind of a two-year-old. "Surely you have a key," the world-famous magician declared.

"Ain't you the lock expert?"

A dagger could not have been sharper than the look Harry Houdini gave in reply to Mr. Bottle's impertinent question.

Houdini drew himself up to his full five feet and six inches. "Kindly deliver this message to Theo Quinn." He bit off each word as if it were coated in cod-liver oil. "If I do not get what I paid for, I will—"

A rattling doorknob stopped the angry declamation. Slowly, the door that had been shut so firmly against the magician, against distractions, against the world, began to creak open. There in a sliver of sunlight stood the object of Houdini's powerful interest.

"So good to see you, Mr. Houdini." A hand was extended to the visitor. Many fingers were adorned with tied bits of string.

Houdini took in the personage standing before him. "*You* are—?"

Dressed in a smart white blouse and navy wool gored skirt, Theodora Quinn completed the world-famous magician's sentence. "The person who will help you vanish an elephant." She gestured toward her study. "I am so sorry to have kept you waiting. Won't you please come in?"

CHAPTER SEVEN

Billy Bottle, Good Samaritan

Billy Bottle watched from the shadows as Mr. Houdini parted company with Theo, possibilities scurrying through his mind like rats through a dark alley. Houdini thought he was Mr. Muckety-Muck, did he? Maybe he'd like to be taken down a notch or two. And Billy was the man to do it.

What Billy heard when he eavesdropped through the vent weren't dull as dirt as Theo's conversations with all them scientist types. This time he could almost follow the conversation, and it perked his spirits up considerable.

Seemed like there was money to be made from Theo's crazy ideas and schemes, if that didn't beat all. A great deal more than the fifteen hundred dollars Mr. Houdini was set to pay her. Though it was a strain on his gray matter, Billy Bottle could parse out that Theo's ideas could be desirable to magicians. But why stop there?

For that matter, why stop with vanishing elephants? If she had figured out how to do that, what else could she vanish? Or whom?

Being so young and book-minded, it would be burdensome for Theo to properly grasp the implications of the opportunities that had ventured her way. It was Billy's duty to relieve her of that burden. And if she didn't see it his way, he had some tricks up his sleeve from the good old days to convince her, did old Billy. He would help Theo envision her full and glittering future. A full and glittering future that did some good for old Billy Bottle himself.

In celebration, the man of the hour let his impressive nose lead him straightaway to the nearest beer hall where he treated himself to a pint and a goodly slab of shepherd's pie.

CHAPTER EIGHT

Insult to Injury

The safest place to conceal herself proved to be one of the baggage cars, and the one in which she'd taken refuge had a fragrant straw-lined floor. The mouse family that had set up housekeeping there soon regretted their decision. Aside from one tiny nibble of a deviled ham sandwich from the picnic hamper, Min had eaten nothing for quite some time. And she did enjoy the clover taste of fresh field mice.

Her picnic complete, Min explored the rest of her surroundings: a jumble of valises, wooden trunks, steamer cases, and crates. Two of the crates contained chickens. Black Orpingtons. Noisy, grumbling biddies apparently determined to keep Min from her post-meal nap. A carefully placed paw through the chicken wire quieted them for a short time, but chickens are not known for long memories. Min barely got herself curled into the perfect position of feline repose before they started nattering again. She was not fluent in Chicken—why ever would one bother to learn? From what she could discern, however, it seemed they were complaining about *her.*

More interesting traveling companions were found in the identical pair of Welsh Corgis on their way to a new home in what they referred to as the Empire City. The dogs tended to finish each other's sentences—they were littermates, after all—but otherwise proved pleasant conversationalists. Are you surprised that cat and canine could and would communicate? Don't be: It is a complete myth that the two species are inevitable enemies. That old rumor was started by a troublemaking parrot.

Like her dear human friend, Min was not well traveled. Still, she was a quick study. For example, despite there being few motorized vehicles making their way to Miss Maisie's, Min had acclimated quickly to the Commodore's touring car, as well as to all the other automobiles rumbling and roaring their way along the streets of the nation's capital. She also had never been to France, but was immediately enchanted by the young woman Audie had brought home from that same trip to Washington, D.C. It does not hurt that the word for *cheese* is the same in Cat as it is in French. Feline and pastry maker were so simpatico that Min had been able to plant the idea about baking *baghlava* in Beatrice's head.

Despite her abilities and intuitions, Min was stymied by the cargo put aboard at the most recent stop. More cage than crate, it took six men to load it into the baggage car. The creature inside was ten times greater than the heft of both Corgis combined and a thousand times more intelligent than the chickens. Min struggled to interpret the new creature's language, reminiscent of Bison, with a hint of Eagle. It didn't help that the language—or perhaps it was the speaker; Min hadn't worked that out yet—was rather nasal in tone. Min *had* worked out that the creature was either *named* Punk or *was* a punk; at least that's what the men had called it. By its limited vocabulary, she had also surmised it was not full-grown. It smelled of hay and apples and something else: The young thing reeked of sorrow. Once the cage had been situated in the baggage car, that smell did more to keep Min awake than all the clucking of those flibbertigibbet hens.

Early on, Min had learned how to comfort little Audie during lonely nights. Min hesitated: Would this baby, huge as it was, also welcome such comforting? If Punk stepped on her, then farewell to one of Min's remaining lives. Yet, she could not bear the creature's melancholy any longer. She padded close, straw shifting and scratching under her paws, to rub her scent against the metal bars of Punk's crate. After a few moments, the creature slowed its rocking. Made a snuffling noise. Min waited, not a muscle twitching. Then something stroked her back through the bars. It was Punk's curious appendage, the one that hung from between his eyes. If it was Punk's nose, it was the most ridiculous nose that Min had ever seen on an animal, but she kept that thought to herself. Hard enough for this baby to be alone; no need to rub salt in the wound by pointing out how homely he was. But then, truthfully, what animal compares to a cat?

"*Moww-rr?*" Min inquired, paw poised in midair.

Punk snuffled again. Puffs of warm air from his long appendage blew tracks in Min's chocolate-striped fur. Min took this as permission and eased slowly between the bars, into the cage, a cage too small for Punk to do anything but stand. She pressed against Punk's front leg and he stopped rocking altogether. Then he slowly eased his solid self into a lean against the metal bars. Min leapt to a spot at the back of Punk's flat head, between ears as big as boat sails. Turning once, twice, three times, she settled herself, purring. Though Punk could not lie down, Min felt him relax.

Min licked at the leathery skin beneath her. It was dry. Punk needed water. Needed rest. Needed . . .

He said something.

Punk said something. And Min understood.

Thank you, he said. *Thank you, friend.*

CHAPTER NINE

I've Been Robbed!

It was all Audie could do to keep her mouth from hanging agape. She felt like a bread crumb being carried along by an army of industrious ants; never had she seen so many people in one place. And all moving with great purpose and determination around her. Her gaze ratcheted upward, taking in the whole of Pennsylvania Station, with its impossibly high walls soaring heavenward, their smooth travertine glowing with warmth. Sunshine flooded through semicircular windows high above, spotlighting the maps painted upon those walls. Audie felt as if she could be lifted completely off her feet by those magnetic sunbeams. In order to remain firmly attached to the ground, she pressed her palms to the cool marble of the Corinthian column by which Cypher had told them to wait. Coming back to her senses a bit, she studied the column. *Was* it Corinthian? Or Ionic? This was yet another subject for further study upon her return home. The library at Miss Maisie's had a small but carefully curated selection of books on architecture.

"Bees and bonnets! Look at those headlines!" Audie released her hold on the stately support.

Bimmy clung to the pillar as if it were a life ring. "Don't wander off," she begged.

Made giddy by the din and aromas and commotion, Audie drifted over to a tidy newsstand steps away. There on the front page was a photograph of Harry Houdini. *Magician Promises to Make Pachyderm Go Poof!* the headline read. She tapped her ear. Was that a buzzing?

"Bimmy, come—" Audie reached out her arm to beckon her friend closer, quite unintentionally but forcefully smacking a complete stranger across the face.

"Ouch!" the victim bellowed, rubbing her cheek.

"I am so sorry!" Audie hastened to apologize to the girl, who wore a canvas bag over a striped dress that was rather lightweight for the crisp March day. "I was motioning to my friend. I didn't see you there."

"Assault and battery." The girl glared at Audie with intense hazel eyes. "I'm gonna call the cops."

"Oh, dear." Audie was loath to begin her stay in New York on such a negative note. Perhaps there was a way to mitigate the situation. "What are you selling?" she inquired, indicating the canvas satchel that appeared to weigh more than the girl.

"You buying?" The hazel eyes squinted.

Audie wiggled her left big toe. She really hoped she wouldn't have to part with her remaining gold coin. She decided to match the girl's tone. "I can't say till I know what you're selling." Audie tried a squint of her own. "And if it's any good."

"Pfft." The girl waggled her left hand, reaching the right into her satchel. "Best sour dills in New York, is all."

"I'll take two." Audie handed over a dime from the pocket money Cypher had given her.

The girl reached into her canvas bag and then stabbed two green spears in Audie's direction. She froze like a deer in the wood when she caught sight of Cypher approaching. "Bone appetite!" she called. In a blink, the pickle vendor disappeared into the crowd.

"You were supposed to stay over there." Cypher pointed. "And what is that?" He looked utterly disgusted.

"Sour pickle." Audie held out the spear. "It's really quite good. Would you like to try a bite?"

"No pickles," he said. "And no more talking to strangers!" How many more times need he repeat this command? Cypher straightened, shoulders back, like any good soldier headed into battle. "Follow me and stay together." He fearlessly led the girls through several grand halls, up sets of grand stairs, and finally through a pair of grand doors.

Outside on the sidewalk, Audie stopped, dumbfounded. Here she was, standing on the streets of New York! The Empire City! Who would have thought it?

"Are you all right?" Bimmy asked.

"Never better, chum!" Audie inhaled deeply of the automobile fumes, the horse dung, the frankfurter carts, the fishy aromas from the Hudson River. "Just smell all that life!" She turned in a complete circle, arms wide, opening herself to the wonders of Manhattan.

Bimmy took a tentative sniff. She tried to prevent it from happening, but the aromas took her instantly to her only other visit to this esteemed city. She and her parents had been performing as trapeze artists: the Flying Forenzas. Papa had allowed *her* to select their stage name. For a moment, Bimmy was back in the big top, knees crimped over a cold metal bar, swinging high above the crowds. *"Zut!"* Papa called, and Bimmy launched herself from the bar, somersaulting through nothingness, until his strong hand caught her up and flipped her over to Mama. Bimmy sniffed again. She did not smell fish or frankfurters or fumes. She smelled her parents.

Audie shook herself out of her big-city reverie to take a close look at her bosom friend. Was that a tear Bimmy was wiping from her eye? "Now, I must ask if you are all right," Audie said.

"Of course." Bimmy made a show of removing a freshly washed and pressed handkerchief from her coat pocket. "Just a bit of ash. City air is so dirty, after all." Bimmy carefully folded the handkerchief and replaced it in her pocket. No reason to weep! Hadn't Papa promised they would be reunited as soon as the run with the Sircus Swisse ended? Why, the five years would pass before she knew it.

Intuiting her younger friend's thoughts, Audie took Bimmy's hand. "I have a feeling this trip will do you real good." She squeezed once, then let go.

Their temporary guardian began instructing a redcap regarding their bags. "Send them to the Evelyn Hotel," Cypher said. "Seven East Twenty-Seventh Street," he added.

The redcap nodded. "Yes, sir."

"Come along, girls." Cypher carried his leather valise in one hand and the wicker picnic basket in the other. He was surprised at the latter's heft, seeing as he and the girls had handily dispatched its contents during their trip. Cypher did not realize that inside said basket lingered a slightly stale piece of *baghlava*, three well-used linen napkins, and one chocolate-striped cat. Min would have been quite cross to know that Cypher found the basket heavy; she'd scarcely consumed enough on the train to keep a kitten alive. The cat pressed her nose to the crack between lid and basket frame, tracking the faint and fading scent of her new friend, Punk. She had promised to look him up in the city, and Min always kept her promises.

Cypher was now ushering the girls into a hansom cab, again announcing their destination.

"You a magician, musician, or bug?" the cab driver inquired.

"Why do you ask?" Cypher's tone turned ominous.

The cabbie shrank back. "Well, the Evelyn's where the troupers usually stay, is all. I didn't mean nothing by it."

"We know you didn't." Audie felt compelled to soften Cypher's remark. She was pleased that she knew what the driver meant by "bug," a term used for an unusual vaudeville act, like paper tearer or sand dancer.

Cypher turned toward her and, instead of scolding, did the most surprising thing. He winked! Audie might've fallen down had she not already been seated in the cab.

"Actually, we are. Troupers, that is." Cypher cleared his throat. "Jugglers. Family act."

Audie's ears perked up. So the entertainment on the train had a purpose, after all!

The cabbie raised his eyebrow but didn't say a word about the unlikelihood of the trio he was transporting being blood kin.

"What's the name of your act?" he asked. "Maybe I'll bring the missus to watch."

"Uh," Cypher coughed. "We are the, the—"

"The Pomegrantos!" Bimmy interjected. "It's Spanish. That's where we're from. *España*."

Audie looked at her friend in amazement. This skill—Audie wouldn't call it lying *exactly*—was one she'd had no idea Bimmy possessed.

"Yes." Cypher's glance at Bimmy was almost appreciative. "The Pomegrantos."

The driver clicked the reins and the horse pulled away from the curb. "What do you think of that, Dobbin?" The horse tossed its head, snorting. "I've hauled me a regular world atlas today. You folks from Spain, and those other folks we brung earlier, they was from Hungary."

A thrill rushed up Audie's spine. "A tiny woman and a very large man?"

The driver clucked his tongue at the horse. "Naw. Brothers, they was. Both 'bout my size."

"Oh." Of course it was too much to hope for another encounter with Madame Volta and Igor; though they had been in contact as of late, letters were not the same. Audie could not help feeling deflated.

"Magicians," the cabbie elaborated. "That Houdini fella is attracting them like flies to a horse pile."

Cypher cleared his throat.

"Beggin' your pardon. I get a bit earthy at times." The driver scratched vigorously under his cap. "Like bees to a hive, I meant to say."

"The picture postcard you sent," Audie murmured. "Houdini."

Cypher put his finger to his lips, and Audie immediately took his meaning.

In a delayed reaction, Bimmy jerked her head toward Cypher. "Did he just say Houdini? Isn't that like the picture—ouch!" She rubbed her side where Audie poked her. Audie then mimicked Cypher's finger-to-mouth gesture.

"Picked up this other magician, too. My last run. The Great Oberon, he called himself." The cabbie now inspected his right nostril with his left forefinger. "Too full of himself, if you ask me."

"Oh, I worked a circus once in Iowa with Oberon. He was lovely," Bimmy said. "Gave me a pet rabbit."

"That doesn't sound like someone who is full of himself," Audie said. "He sounds kind."

The cabbie clucked to the horse by way of answer.

"What happened to your rabbit?" Audie wondered aloud. Bimmy had arrived at Miss Maisie's pet-free.

"Oh, I let Hoppy go in the woods near Cedar Rapids. Sometimes circus animals aren't treated very nice." A pained look flitted across Bimmy's face. "I wanted him to have a happy, rabbity life."

"What a good heart you have, Bim." Audie snuggled close, both out of affection and out of a need for warmth. It was a raw day.

The horse clip-clopped south on Seventh, turning on Twenty-Seventh to follow the long avenues, until, after crossing Fifth Avenue, the cabbie called out, "Whoa, there, Dobbin." They stopped mid-block, apparently arrived.

Cypher assisted the shivering girls down from the cab, then

pulled out his wallet. "Hurry inside, to the lobby, where it's warmer." Audie was grateful for Cypher's thoughtfulness but wondered in that moment if their pickle friend had anyone finding a warm spot for *her*.

Bimmy tugged her out of her reverie. "Onward, chum!"

The lobby of the Evelyn Hotel was nowhere near as majestic as Pennsylvania Station but exuded an energy and charm of its own. It bustled with performers of all shapes and sizes, from the smallest man Audie had ever seen to the largest woman. And was that a mermaid across the way? It was difficult to know where to look in this three-ring circus of a reception area. The walls themselves were pasted, floor to ceiling, with posters of vaudeville acts, major and minor.

"Oh, look, Bimmy." Audie moved to inspect a particular poster. "There's your friend, the Great Oberon."

Bimmy perused the placard over Audie's shoulder. "That's him doing his best-known trick," she said. "The Asrah Levitation."

"You know him, do you?" the desk clerk commented, obviously listening in on the girls' conversation. "I expect he'll pop into the lobby here right quick." The clerk nodded at the mantel clock nearby. "Mail's just come." He indicated a set of cubbyholes, some with keys in them, some with slips of paper, and some empty. "He must be expecting something important. He's down here every fifteen minutes like clockwork." He chuckled vigorously at his feeble joke.

"Is Mr. Houdini also a guest here?" Audie wondered if that was why Cypher had selected this hotel.

The clerk threw back his bald head and roared. "Houdini? If he leaves his home in Harlem, it's to stay in the Ritz, not joints like this!"

Cypher strode up to the desk, his presence quickly quieting the laughter. He took a fountain pen from the desk and signed them all in.

"A message for you, sir," the clerk said upon reading the register. He presented Cypher with an envelope. Audie tried to peek at it but Cypher too quickly slipped it into his vest pocket.

Audie was not well traveled, but she grasped that the Evelyn was nothing like the Ardmore, her accommodations in the nation's capital. *That* hotel had required a chaperone for a young girl on her own. It would seem the Evelyn was not nearly so particular. And how could it be, what with so many theatrical children running around? Audie was fairly certain the impish boy in the corner was Eddie Foy, of the Seven Little Foys, whose poster hung directly above Cypher's head.

The clerk handed over two keys. "I don't have adjoining, but you can be dye-rectly across the hall from your . . . nieces." He took the bills Cypher handed him and placed them in a drawer. "And no pets unless they're cleared first. I've already got ten dogs, five monkeys, and a seal." The clerk took a nip from a bottle tightly wrapped in a brown paper sack. "Enough to give a man an ulcer." He smacked his lips.

"Upstairs, girls." Cypher pointed to the elevator.

Audie hesitated. "But what about our things?"

"The bellman will bring them." Cypher jingled the keys in his hand. "Do you prefer even or odd?"

Bimmy's face clouded with confusion, but Audie brightly answered, "Odd."

"Then it's room 513 for you." He handed her one key and pocketed the other. "I'll be in 514."

They stepped across to the elevator. The door slid open and a man in a rumpled brown suit dashed out, nearly bowling Audie over.

"Help, someone!" he cried. "I've been robbed!"

CHAPTER TEN

Mail Call

Violet skipped back from the mailbox. Mr. Scattergood, the postman, had let her feed Jewell a sugar cube. The horse's lips had moved soft and velvety against Violet's palm, a sensation that sent a jolt of such happiness through her that not even Divinity's sudden appearance spoiled her mood.

"I'll take those." Divinity blocked Violet's path.

The eldest triplet promptly handed over the packet of letters. She was still bruised from the nasty pinch Divinity had meted out for not passing the potatoes quickly enough. As she placed the last of the mail in Divinity's outstretched hand, Violet exclaimed, "Why, there's a letter for you!"

Mail for the Waywards was not an unknown occurrence, but it was rare. It seemed that most parents lost interest in communicating with their daughters once they'd been placed in Miss Maisie's care. In their young lives, Violet and her sisters had had three missives from their family, precious letters that they reread on their shared birthday. As far back as Violet could remember, she could not recall Divinity ever receiving mail.

Divinity squinted at Violet as if to measure whether or not she was playing a prank. She glanced down at the envelope in her hands. "Why, so it is!" She slipped it into her pinafore pocket, then hurried to deliver the remainder of the post to Miss Maisie. For once, she did not stop to accept a sweet from her headmistress, nor commiserate with Miss Maisie as she wondered aloud where her invitation to lunch with Mrs. So-and-So had got to. "The mail service these days," muttered Miss Maisie.

"Yes, it is nice, isn't it?" answered Divinity, before running off to her favorite spot, the sunporch window seat, next to the potted cacti. She could tell by both the return address and the penmanship that this letter was not from either of her parents. Her mother tended to add a little swirl to the "y" at the close of Divinity's name, and her father's hand was nearly illegible. This script appeared to be taken from a penmanship practice book, it was that neat and tidy.

Divinity ran her forefinger under the flap of the envelope, prying it open. Inside was nestled a sheaf of rich letterhead, soft as butter, covered with that same neat and tidy script. She pulled it out, pressing it smooth before reading.

The letter was short but rich with revelations.

"My, my." Divinity rested letter in lap with trembling hands. She never knew she had a great-uncle named Woebegone Thompson. Nor that he had a farm in Upstate New York. Near Elmira.

She reread the carefully penned words several more times, trying to take them in. *Last Will and Testament. Woebegone's Way. Forty acres.* All hers. Free and clear.

Divinity sat very still, contemplating the alarming news. Another one of the Waywards might have rejoiced at the letter's contents. Freedom at last! But not Divinity. Among her many flaws was one most glaring: a distinct lack of an imagination. She had no desire to do anything more than to run Miss Maisie's School. Someday. For now, Divinity was content to play the tyrant of the Waywards.

She slipped the letter back into the envelope and then into her pocket, determined not to reveal its contents to a soul. She was confident Violet would never tell anyone about the letter, being so tender-skinned and all.

Though the other Waywards had complained on many occasions to Divinity about her habit of talking aloud in her sleep, she never paid them any attention. It didn't keep her awake, so why should she be concerned? Thus Divinity had no idea that, a few nights later while Miss Maisie's thirteen other wards soundly slept, she betrayed *herself*, revealing all through middle-of-the-night whispers and mumbles.

And Divinity also had no idea that one set of Wayward ears heard everything.

CHAPTER ELEVEN

No Way to Treat a Baby

Helmut, the elephant trainer, checked the heavy manacle around the punk's leg.

His assistant winced to see that the metal had already chafed a raw spot on the young creature's flesh. "Seems a bit tight," he commented.

Helmut spit into the hay. "He'll learn faster that way." The trainer grunted. This new assistant—Jamie Doolan, was it?—had soft notions. These beasts responded best to fear, to pain, not to kindness. The sooner Jamie learned that, the better.

The Shubert brothers, owners of the Hippodrome, had noticed the immense popularity of the Powers' elephants and decided to have an elephant for their very own. This infant male had come on the market and they'd snatched him up, named him Baby. Helmut was to teach him to pass out programs at the front entrance. Before learning any tricks, however, Baby needed to learn who was boss. Helmut would make certain of that.

The little elephant tugged and tugged but could not remove himself from the restraint. He sounded an alarm, struggling even harder. Helmut raised his arm, wielding the sharpened bull hook. Jamie Doolan flinched, turning his face away. He could not watch.

Already familiar with the punishment device in the head trainer's hand, Baby stopped his struggling.

"See?" Helmut's grin was more sneer than anything. "It's the only thing the dumb creatures understand." He tossed the bull hook to Jamie, who fumbled to catch it.

Jamie looked around the stall deep in the bowels of the Hippodrome. "I'll muck this out then feed him, shall I?" He'd no experience with elephants, but had worked odd jobs at the Star stables uptown.

"Don't you know anything?" The accusation exploded from the trainer. "No food for at least three days. He has to learn." Helmut turned on his heel. "I'll be tending to Jennie if you need help."

Trembling in his too-large boots, Jamie watched the head trainer go. He'd thought *he* had it bad, back there in the state home for orphans. Despite the questionable quality of the meals, at least he got fed on a regular basis.

Baby blew a note through his trunk that sounded as sad as any Jamie had ever heard. He set the bull hook in the corner, then approached the cage slowly.

"Buck up, Baby." He stroked the young elephant's trunk. "I'll be keeping an eye on you." From each jacket pocket he pulled an apple, which the elephant dispatched with lightning speed. Then his talented trunk tapped at Jamie's pants pocket. Jamie laughed.

"You want more, do you? Greedy little thing." He glanced around. Helmut was preoccupied with Jennie and her sisters.

"I'll be back right quick," Jamie assured the elephant. He slipped out the loading door and, there where he remembered it, he found the pushcart selling produce. Jamie haggled with the peddler and soon his pockets were full of bruised and rotting fruit, bought at bargain prices. Or so Jamie thought.

"Always glad to do business with a *schlemiel*." The peddler tipped his cap.

"Good day to you, too!" Jamie replied, unaware he'd been insulted. He hurried back with his purchases. He'd have to be sly about feeding Baby, but Jamie was used to being sly. That was one skill he'd perfected in the orphanage. With luck, Helmut wouldn't know a thing.

Baby downed the rutabagas and oranges and carrots with enthusiasm. Between each course, he exhaled happily, flapping his ears. Without even realizing it, Jamie sang "Hush Ye, My Bairnie" as the baby elephant ate. The tune came natural, it did. Though his da was Irish, his ma was Scottish. She was the one to sing lullabies to him. And it was with that song he used to lull his baby sis to sleep, before . . .

When Baby had eaten every last bit of flesh, seed, and rind, he wrapped his trunk around Jamie's arm, as if to pull him into the cage.

"I'll use that hook on *him*." Jamie tossed his head in Helmut's direction. "If he ever even thinks of taking it to you again."

Then he grabbed a shovel and, whistling, mucked out Baby's stall.

CHAPTER TWELVE

Mysteries and Magicians

A crowd gathered around the rumpled man in brown, whom Audie now recognized from the train.

"What's missing?" someone asked.

"Has anyone called the police?" interjected another voice.

The large lady waved her enormous arms. "Give the poor fellow some air!" There was sufficient authority in her voice and girth that the crowd ebbed, and the rumpled man stood alone in the center, like the cheese in "The Farmer in the Dell."

To Audie's surprise, Cypher did not step forward to offer professional assistance; rather, he edged away from the commotion. She took a cue from his behavior, towing Bimmy with her.

"Take a breath," the large lady suggested. "And start at the beginning."

The man shuddered, a bit overdramatically to Audie's mind. But these were theater people after all; perhaps that was to be expected. "I was gathering my props for an audition." He smoothed his luxurious imperial moustache with a trembling hand. "At the Hippodrome."

The crowd murmured appreciatively at this honor.

Someone handed the man a glass of water, which he gratefully accepted. Sipped. Spoke again. "Then I was called to the telephone, on the second floor."

"They need phones on every floor," someone grumbled.

The man continued, patting his forehead with a dingy handkerchief. "It had to have happened while I was taking the telephone call. My trunk hasn't been out of my sight otherwise."

"What was taken?" one of the acrobats asked, evidently eager to get to the punch line.

"Everything!" The man drained the glass, and water beaded up the fringes of his moustache. "At least, everything I need for the Asrah Levitation. What am I to do?"

"Your signature trick!" The large woman's hand flew to her ample bosom in shock.

A murmur wobbled its way through the crowd.

The Great Oberon nodded slowly, solemnly. "I suspect a fellow magician," he confessed in a tone veering on tragic. "Jealous of my audition at the Hippodrome."

"Lemme through!" A beat cop weaved through the crowded lobby, clearing a path to the Great Oberon. "Back about your own business," he commanded, pushing the odd performer this way and that. "Are you the fella's missing a cape?"

"Not a cape." The Great Oberon tugged his waistcoat, insulted. "The props for my grandest illusion."

The policeman gave him a funny look.

"Trick," clarified Oberon. "I make my assistant levitate."

Again the policeman looked puzzled.

"I make someone float in midair." The Great Oberon threw his hands up in exasperation.

"Oh, do you now? That might be worth the price of admission." The officer cocked his head. "You'd best come with me and tell my sergeant all about it." At that instruction, the Great Oberon fetched hat, gloves, and overcoat and then followed the policeman out of the hotel.

"How terrible," Audie said. "Stealing someone's trick like that."

Bimmy was uncharacteristically quiet. Audie reminded herself that her best chum was new at this adventure game. She was bound to feel overwhelmed and out of her league, the poor thing.

"It's a competitive business," explained Cypher. "And it actually illustrates why we've been hired." He corrected himself. "Why *I've* been hired to—"

"Keep an eye on me," a pleasant voice finished.

Cypher's face paled at the sight of the young woman at his elbow, dressed in a crisp white bodice and gored navy wool skirt. She held out an ink-stained hand. Audie counted six bits of string tied around assorted fingers. "Theodora Quinn," she said, by way of introduction. "But do call me Theo."

Cypher was grateful the bellman had not yet taken their bags up. He was going to need the headache powders in his valise. Perhaps a double dose. This was not part of the plan. In fact, this young woman wasn't to have known she was being . . . watched. How did she find out? And how did she find him? Mr. Pinkerton was not going to be happy about this. Not in the least bit. Nor was Mr. Houdini.

Perhaps they'd take him back on at the White House.

Cypher cleared his throat, glancing around the still bustling lobby. "I assume you are the young woman who will be auditioning for our troupe?" he asked.

"Well, Mr. Hou—"

"*Zut!*" As if from thin air, Cypher conjured a trio of silk scarves and tossed them to the young woman.

Audie blinked. How could a person's hands move that fast?

Miss Quinn caught the scarves in a messy clump. "*Zut?*"

"It's a circus phrase," Bimmy explained. "It can mean 'Are you ready?' or 'Let's go!'" She pressed her palms together, thinking. "Or just about anything, really."

"Of course, as a performer yourself, you are well aware of that," Audie said brightly.

"We have very high standards," Cypher continued. "We would not want someone inexperienced holding us back."

Gamely, the young woman tossed the scarves into the air, one after another.

"Oh, very good," Audie cheered, when she saw that neither Bimmy nor Cypher was going to encourage Miss Quinn. Who, clearly, had not sought them out with the intent of auditioning for a role in the Pomegrantos. Though brief to date, Audie's experience with the rescue business had been lengthy enough to recognize when someone needed saving. Case in point: Miss Quinn. And why was that scruffy-looking man with the fantastically large nose lurking behind the potted philodendron? He seemed to be taking a great interest in the current conversation.

"Is there somewhere quiet we can go?" Audie asked. "To continue the . . . audition?"

Cypher bristled at Audie's apparent attempt to take charge of the situation. Then he, too, caught sight of the nosy man. "I have identified a café around the corner that will provide some privacy."

"Brilliant!" Theo exclaimed. "Because I'm starving. I completely forgot to eat yesterday." She reflected a moment, her chocolate-drop eyes large behind the round spectacles a bit askew on her nose, as she studied the wiggling fingers she held up in front of her face. "And perhaps this morning as well."

After a short walk to the café, the party was soon seated in a booth, lunches ordered for all except Cypher, who merely drank coffee. Many cups. When the food arrived, the girls tucked in. Audie herself was famished, but did offer Cypher a bite of her apple pie à la mode, which he declined.

"Quite right," Audie conceded. "Not as tasty as anything Beatrice whips up."

Cypher did not comment.

The girls' mealtime conversation was lively and educational, thanks to Theodora Quinn.

"You are a whiz!" Audie's head was spinning from Theo's explanation of her latest experiment. Something to do with light and refractions.

"I can take this off since I've now eaten. Though I could manage a second piece of pie." Theo removed a string from one finger. "I am a whiz at many things," she admitted without a hint of boastfulness. "Things scientific. But people completely mystify me." She picked up a piecrust crumb with her forefinger and put it in her mouth. "Mr. Houdini, for example. I am a nobody. Why would he hire you to protect me?"

"I cannot imagine whatever gave you that idea." Cypher did his best to don a shocked expression.

"Not whatever." Theo arched her brow. "Whomever. As in Mr. Houdini himself."

Cypher blanched. Why on earth would his employer reveal such information? "I am not at liberty—"

"Maybe Mr. Houdini felt Theo's being fully informed was her best protection?" Audie suggested.

Another small dose of headache powders disappeared into Cypher's mouth. "It would be much more efficient if those not involved in the safety and security business left it to those of us who are so involved." That was the last critical thing he would say of Mr. Houdini. Though Cypher could foresee himself *thinking* a great many more.

"But I'm a scientist," Theo protested. "From whom could I possibly be in danger?"

Cypher's only answer was to take another sip of coffee. When the waitress refilled his cup, he ordered another slice of pie for Theodora Quinn.

Audie felt she must show the more cooperative side of their team. "I do not mean to alarm you, but there are those in Mr. Houdini's profession who will resort to drastic measures to ensure their own success. Why, moments ago, the Great Oberon was a victim of an unthinkable robbery. Likely committed by a jealous competitor. Isn't that right, Bimmy?"

"About that—" Bimmy began.

"The police did not confirm the robbery," Cypher cautioned. "Take care when it comes to the word of a vaudeville performer."

"A robbery?" Theo Quinn pushed her spectacles up the bridge of her nose. "What was pilfered?"

Audie pondered Cypher's remark. "You mean it might be like the time Miss Maisie was certain her butterfly brooch had been stolen and all the while it was behind her dressing table?"

Cypher rubbed his temples. This conversation was rapidly sliding out of his control. "May I repeat—"

"A prop for his most important trick," Audie explained to Theo. "His signature illusion."

"About that—" Bimmy began again.

Cypher slapped his hand on the café table. Dishes rattled. Diners around them stared. Cypher inhaled. Composed himself. "No more robbery talk."

Bimmy also inhaled, sitting up in her seat. She edged a bit closer to Audie for security and support. "There is *one* thing I should say on the topic."

The waitress approached with a slice of pie.

Cypher's hand waved "no."

"Oh, you didn't want this after all?" the waitress said.

Cypher groaned.

"Here, please." Theo patted the space in front of her. "Oh, cherry. My favorite!"

"Dear Cypher," Audie pleaded. "Do let Bimmy speak her mind." She noticed her good friend had eaten around her meal, not of it. And she hadn't even touched a bite of dessert. Though not up to Beatrice's standards, the meal on the whole was quite enjoyable. This lack of enthusiasm was not like Bimmy, who generally had a hearty appetite.

Cypher gritted his teeth and sat back. He was going to have to stock up on headache powders. There was no doubt about it. Fortunately, he'd seen a pharmacy on the opposite corner. "Go on, then." A muscle in his jaw twitched.

Bimmy tugged on the dark curl over her right ear. "Oberon wasn't robbed."

"You see, I warned you about jumping to conclusions," Cypher said.

"Oberon wasn't robbed because that wasn't Oberon." Bimmy put her hands in her lap.

Audie's fork clattered to her plate. "What?"

Cypher closed his eyes, as if in prayer. "Ladies, if I may—"

"Oh, this is so thrilling!" Theo clapped gleefully. "I must get out of my laboratory more often."

Bimmy glanced at Audie and then at Cypher. "Do you remember in the cab I told you Oberon and I had performed in the same circus?"

"Oh yes!" Audie's eyes sparkled with the memory. "He gave you a rabbit. Which you set free in the woods."

"Clever girl," Theo approved. "Animals deserve to live in their natural environments. I myself once rehabilitated a small barred owl. Though it does return to my window from time to time, it seems to have fully embraced its natural state. Quite remarkable, really."

Cypher rubbed at his temples with vigor. "This is all fascinating, but might we return to the subject at hand?" Keeping a conversation on track with these three was more difficult than herding camels!

"Yes. Well." Bimmy rearranged her silverware just so. "At first, I hesitated to say anything. You see, it's not uncommon on the circuit for performers to fill in for one another. Once when Papa contracted the influenza, Monsieur Reynaud took over. Though he wasn't as handsome as Papa or as skilled at aerobatics, the audience did not know the difference. Mr. Oberon often suffered from something Mama and Papa called the 'bottle flu.' There were many, many times he could not perform because of this illness." Bimmy reached for her milk glass and sipped. "So it wouldn't be that unusual for another magician to step in for the Great Oberon and assume his role." She glanced from Audie to Theo to Audie again. "It happens more often than you might realize, especially on the road."

"Completely fascinating." Theo took out a small notepad. "And no one ever notices these substitutions?"

Cypher stirred another spoonful of sugar into his coffee, clicking the spoon energetically against the cup. He had been about to ask that very question. And he said so.

"No." Bimmy shook her head. "Since we're often only in one town for a day or so, it's not likely anyone in the audience would know whether the Great Oberon was tall or short, fat or thin." Her shoulders slid ear-ward. "A good performer can don another persona as easily as one dons a costume."

"But, Bimmy, dear," Audie interjected. "Something must be different about *this* substitution. Or why would you even note it?"

Once again Bimmy reached for her milk as if to sip. "It doesn't add up. What he said." She set the glass down, brows crinkling. "A magician's trunk generally goes straight to the theater. Being so heavy and all." She nibbled at a bit of piecrust. "Not to the hotel."

"What a sharp mind!" Theo exclaimed. "Have you ever thought about immersing yourself in the natural or physical sciences?"

"I beg your pardon?"

"She thinks you'd make a wonderful scientist," Audie clarified. "And I wholeheartedly agree."

"I have room in my laboratory for an assistant," offered Theo.

"You mean, come here to work?" Bimmy's face paled.

"Not much monetary reward," admitted Theo. "But there is always the chance to change the world."

"Oh, I couldn't leave Audie! And the Waywards!" Even as she voiced these declarations, Bimmy felt intrigued. A scientist! My, my. "At least not now."

Theo smiled warmly. "The invitation is open-ended," she said.

Cypher drained his coffee cup. His vision flickered slightly due to excessive caffeine. He blinked. Twice. Now there was the proper number of girls. "I believe we should leave the faux Mr. Oberon to the police and concentrate on the matters at hand."

Audie was distressed to notice she had absolutely devoured every bite of her meal. There was not even the smallest bit of pie remaining. *Quel dommage*, as Beatrice would say. Regardless, Audie pressed on. "And what are the matters at hand?"

Cypher glanced around, lowering his voice. "I hadn't planned on sharing this information with Miss Quinn—"

"Oh, do call me Theo."

"With Miss Quinn. No sense causing unnecessary worry." Cypher pulled a piece of paper from his vest pocket. "But Mr. Houdini hired me because he was worried about something along these lines." He showed the crude letter to the girls. "He received this yesterday."

"Bees and bonnets!" Audie surmised this was the envelope that Cypher had been given at the hotel. She read the letter, taking in the threats on the page. "Kidnap Theo? But why?"

"Given what you've said about the Great Oberon, I believe I can answer that." Theo reached across the table to pat Audie's hand. "You see, I have designed for Mr. Houdini one of his most ambitious and—if I may be allowed a modicum of conceit—most amazing illusions." She shifted in her chair, glancing left and right. "I am the one who will help him disappear an elephant."

Audie's pie sat leaden in her stomach. She wrestled with a dual set of potent emotions: curiosity about such a feat and anxiety at the topic of elephants. After all, these were the very creatures that, while stampeding, had taken the lives of her dear parents.

As if intuiting Audie's inner turmoil, Bimmy placed her hand on her chum's shoulder.

Audie composed herself. "I saw that in the newspaper at Pennsylvania Station." She turned to Theo. "I suppose it would violate some ancient code if you were to tell us how such a thing might happen."

"You are wise beyond your years." Theo swallowed her last bite of pie. "I cannot tell you. Nor will I tell anyone. Not even if I am kidnapped." She lifted her chin and spoke firmly and bravely to Cypher. "Or worse."

Cypher leaned forward. "Well—"

"You have nothing to worry about!" interrupted Audie. "Cypher will keep you safe. And, if I may say so, I am quite useful in kidnapping cases."

"I am in good hands, then," Theo declared.

Audie sat up proudly. "The best."

"All shall be well," Cypher assured her. "As long as you do exactly as we say." He explained the complex plan he had concocted for keeping her safe, a plan that involved Theo joining the Pomegrantos. Their juggling rehearsals would provide the opportunity for Theo and Mr. Houdini to be at the Hippodrome at the same time. Cypher explained how Mr. Houdini had arranged for Theo to confer with him in private to finalize the illusion's last details. At the end of his lengthy dissertation, Cypher ran a hand through his handsome dark hair. "And there is one more thing."

"Name it!" Theo Quinn's eyes sparkled like jewels behind her spectacles.

Cypher rubbed the bridge of his nose. Even with Mr. Houdini's endorsement, the Pomegrantos' act still needed to meet certain standards. "You will need to improve your juggling skills."

Theo moved a string from her ring finger to her forefinger. "Absolutely."

CHAPTER THIRTEEN

Finding Punk

Min wiggled to freedom while the man was in the washroom down the hall. She'd feared she'd be trapped in that basket forever. First, there'd been all that commotion downstairs, and then her humans had disappeared for a goodly while. Unconfined at last, Min gave herself a good shake from nose to rump and then twitched her tail twice. The door to room 514 cracked open enough for the cat to wriggle through to the hallway. With another tail twitch the door softly closed behind her. The cat's keen nose led her directly across the worn carpet to another door, which, with a third tail twitch, was soon ajar. Her charges, still in their travel clothes, were curled together on the bed like a litter of kittens. She sniffed around Audie and the other girl until she was reassured of their safety and well-being. They were no doubt exhausted from their long journey and that excitement in the lobby. Quite a to-do over what? A sheet and some wire? As Min had observed on countless occasions, humans have a tendency to overreact.

She leapt to the windowsill, the window itself left ajar out of habit by her best human friend. Min's ears pricked up as she took stock of the situation. It would take five or six leaps to reach the street. With a last glance over her chocolate-striped shoulder at the girls, out she went, landing as confidently as ever on four snow-white paws.

The city smells threatened to confuse her—rat-scented steam from someplace deep below, shad and striped bass from a close-by river, and the ever-present stench of humans. Fortunately, she'd had several days on the train to get well attuned to Punk's scent. She padded past dry goods stores, underneath fruit and vegetable displays, around street peddlers pushing carts heaped with wares, until she found the building she sought. Despite being in the shadow of the Sixth Avenue El, it loomed like an enormous perched owl, absorbing the entire block between Forty-Third and Forty-Fourth Streets. Min ducked into an entryway, Punk's scent leading her on.

She skittered around workers carrying velvet drapes and wooden boards and lengths of rope; none seemed to see her, or if they did, chose to take no notice. She could not know that they were glad for the cat's presence; all the feed and animal waste in the deep recesses of the theater attracted rats. And if there was one thing stage workers detested, it was rats.

Oblivious to the workers' hopes, the cat forged ahead, motivated by one reason only: the sad aroma signaling her new friend, Punk. She turned down a dark hallway, and down a darker set of stairs. Ahead was an enormous door behind which bubbled a stew of animal scents, including that of the baby she sought.

With purpose, Min padded forward.

Only to be stopped by a snarling pair of Dobermans.

* CHAPTER FOURTEEN *

The Pomegrantos

"Very nice," Bert, the stage manager, *lied at the conclusion of the family's* performance. What were they called? Bert consulted his clipboard. The Pomegrantos. Real oilcans, duds. And the show hardly needed another set of jugglers! Their costumes weren't bad; eye-catching even, with that bright trim and lacing. No matter. If it were up to him, he'd send them packing. But Mr. Houdini asked for them special. And Bert did enjoy getting paid on a regular basis. He'd be pink-slipped for certain if he didn't do as Mr. Houdini asked.

"I think we've got room for you." Bert was practically convincing. "Real nice spot, too. Next-to-closing." He had a feeling these green-horns would have no idea they'd just been given the worst spot.

"Oh, thank you. Thank you!" The funny little slip of a girl with the wild auburn curls grabbed hands with her "sisters" and they all did a little jig.

Bert chewed on the unlit cigar in his mouth. The father or brother or whoever he was should consider going out as a single—he was the only one of the act who could juggle worth beans, though the littlest girl wasn't bad. The gal with the glasses was completely hopeless. And what gave with all those strings tied around her fingers? Absolutely off-putting. Bert made a note on his clipboard to have mops ready. The Pomegrantos were likely to be on the receiving end of some rotten tomatoes during the rowdier matinees. "Come with me to my office," he said to Cypher. "I'll write up your contract."

"Wait here," Cypher instructed the girls.

"We wouldn't dream of going elsewhere," Theo replied. She was completely bewitched by the ropes and pulleys backstage and found the perfect spot in the wings from which to watch the grips at work. "Fascinating," she muttered, reaching for her notebook. She was soon sketching away, filling page after page.

The younger girls watched the remainder of the rehearsal, especially enjoying a tumbling team from England and a trained seal act; they were not as enamored of the opera singer.

Audie covered her ears as the diva hit a high C.

"When do you think Mr. Houdini will arrive?" she asked. The first run-through for the Vanishing Elephant illusion was set for that very afternoon. There were only three days till it debuted in front of thousands.

"Look there." Bimmy tapped Audie's shoulder. "Isn't that him?"

The girls turned, mesmerized. The world-famous magician swooped onto the enormous stage. In his wake trotted a small terrier wearing a proud expression. Though Mr. Houdini was not much taller than Theo, he carried himself as if he matched height with Abe Lincoln. He strode, chin up, chest out, shoulders back, like royalty. And indeed he was. Royalty in the world of magicians. Mr. Will Rogers had called Houdini the greatest showman of the times.

Audie thrilled to see him in person and couldn't wait for the opportunity to tell the Waywards all about it. She determined to write a postcard that very evening. Audie put on her warmest smile, anticipating his passing their way, speaking to Theo, though the girl scientist was completely distracted with those backstage gizmos. Perhaps Theo would introduce her "sisters" to the great man. Audie rehearsed what she might say: "It is a sincere pleasure to meet you, sir." Would a curtsy be out of order? He was royalty, after all.

Audie cleared away her dreamy thoughts. Mr. Houdini could not acknowledge Theo! That would be folly. No one must suspect their connection. That would not only put the illusion at risk, but Theo as well.

Of course, Mr. Houdini did not stride backstage to greet Theo, and thus Audie was not formally introduced to the world-famous magician. He talked for some time and in a rather loud voice to one of the stagehands. Something about sugar cubes and wagon wheels and sufficient men to pull an elephant. Then, with a flourish, he spun away, his red-satin-lined cape swirling dramatically about him. "I'll be in my dressing room," he was heard to say.

Theo smoothed her skirt after tucking her notebook into a hidden pocket in the right side seam. "That's my cue," she said to Audie, in a low tone. "In ten minutes, I am to pretend I am delivering a note—" She pulled one such from the left skirt pocket. "And then, in the privacy of his dressing room, we will go over the latest revisions to—"

Bimmy leapt into action, landing hard on the toe of Theo's boot. From Audie's perspective, it appeared that Bimmy had intentionally engaged in this unkind act.

"Bimmy, dear!" Theo exclaimed, hopping on the uninjured appendage, while rubbing the smited one. "Do watch where you step!"

"Oh, hello!" Bimmy's voice was loud and fraught with tension. She mouthed an apology to Theo all the while twitching her head backstage. Bimmy had spent much of her young life in the circus, absorbing enough to know that, in show business, large ears lurked everywhere. And Theo's recent conversation was not for public consumption.

"How are you today?" Bimmy continued to speak to the heavy curtain.

The rumpled man emerged from behind thick velvet, blinking in the transition from dark to light. "Do I know you?" There was an undercurrent of suspicion and irritation to his question.

Bimmy froze. On her reply hinged much.

"We know your reputation," she answered smoothly. Her glibness continued to be an inspiration to Audie. "And we're on the bill here. *Next to last.*"

"*Humph.*" The Great Oberon could not be bothered with kid acts. And certainly not kid acts holding the least desirable spot on the bill. He fussed with his moustache in irritation.

Audie's ear buzz caused her to recall a similar sensation on the train. A sensation she had dismissed due to railway noise. Perhaps she had been too hasty in her conclusion.

"Sisters," Bimmy said with forced enthusiasm. "Isn't it an honor to be in the same room with the Great Oberon?"

Theo set her injured foot down. "Oh my, yes, *sister.*"

"It is a genuine pleasure, sir." Audie dipped into a curtsy, grateful for their stage makeup and garish costumes; she did not think it would be in their best interest if "Mr. Oberon" recognized them from either the train or hotel.

"Where is Bert?" was Mr. Oberon's only reply. "We were to have an audition! Find him!"

Bimmy and Audie scurried away to obey the command, leaving Theo to limp off to her assignation with Mr. Houdini. The younger girls met Bert as he and Cypher returned from the business office where the performance contract had been signed. Bert was blowing his nose and rubbing red-rimmed eyes. Cypher wore a bewildered expression, which Audie could not read. She could not know that he was puzzling over Bert's advice not to send their laundry out. Cypher had thanked him, of course, for the wise words, completely unaware that Bert was telling him, in vaudevillian lingo, that he didn't think the act would even go the full week.

"Mr. Oberon is requesting an audience with you," Audie informed the stage manager. "For the audition."

Bert sneezed again. He knew he was allergic to cats, but was he also allergic to magicians? Why else would he be sneezing so? "Where is he?" he asked.

"Over—" Audie turned, then stopped. "Well, he was right there." She gently shook her head. It seemed perhaps that the buzzing was dying down.

"He'll find me." Bert put his thumbs under his suspenders. "Don't worry."

"Do tell him we delivered his message." Audie did not want any bad blood with Mr. Oberon, or whoever he was.

"He was most insistent," Bimmy added.

Bert sneezed again and made a mental note to buy another bottle of Dr. Leo's Breathene syrup. Those magicians: Give them a top hat, cape, and magic wand and they thought they ruled the world. "Be here for rehearsals in the morning," he told Cypher, stifling a sneeze. "It's a five-dollar fine if you're late."

"Five dollars!" Cyper exclaimed. It was becoming increasingly clear that vaudeville was a racket. Five-dollar late fees. Two-dollar union fees. Fifty cents for the stagehand memorial fund. How did a person make a living in this world? He was about to launch into a well-thought-out but pointed tirade when Audie stopped him with a tug on the arm.

"Come meet Herring." She and Bimmy led him backstage. They passed a young man in a battered cap as he put something in his jacket pocket. Audie paused and he caught her gaze. She tugged on Cypher's arm. Even though her ear was not buzzing, something about the young man didn't add up. The minute she made that move, the young man was gone.

"Was there something you needed?" Cypher asked.

Audie glanced left and right. Had she really seen the lad? "No," she said slowly. "Nothing." She brightened. "Except for you to say hello to Herring!"

Cypher pinched his nose by way of introduction. Seals are rather aromatic creatures, what with all the fish they consume. To the girls' delight, Herring's trainer allowed them to serve his lunch. The seal was especially fond of herring, thus his name.

"Wayuh is Deo?" Cypher's query through his pinched nose made him sound as if he were speaking underwater.

Bimmy's head tilted toward the dressing rooms.

"With you-know-who." Audie wiped a bit of herring guts from her fingers. "I'm sure she'll be along directly."

Three of the Pomegrantos spent the next half hour getting acquainted with their fellow performers. Bimmy was especially taken with one young English acrobat named Archibald Leach, who gave her a toffee in exchange for a tumbling lesson.

The three partners were so engaged in conversation—trade talk, if you will—that there was no comment when Mr. Houdini passed by them again, that charming fox terrier at his heel. Sans cape, Mr. Houdini was less theatrical, but still Audie felt honored to be in his presence.

The great magician stood at the fringes of the gathered group, apparently too proud to join in with the lesser performers. He caught Cypher's eye and motioned him near. Cypher complied. Audie and Bimmy followed at a discreet distance so as not to call attention.

"It's half past two," the great magician observed.

"Yes." Cypher nodded. "Nearly time for the first run-through of the illusion." He patted his pockets. Full of sugar cubes as Mr. Houdini had requested. Jennie the elephant was evidently inordinately fond of sugar.

"You seem remarkably unconcerned." Houdini rocked back and forth on his well-polished shoes.

Cypher's face folded into a question mark. "Unconcerned?"

Though actors and stagehands and hangers-on were milling about, causing sufficient commotion to cover the conversation, Houdini lowered his voice. "The object that was to be delivered an hour ago," he said, eyebrow raised, as if offering a clue.

Still Cypher wore a confused expression.

Audie racked her brain to decipher the magician's comments. Object. An hour ago. "Oh!" she gasped. "But it *was* delivered!"

Bimmy's confusion now matched Cypher's.

"Our *sister*." Audie rolled her hands as if to stir her colleagues' memories. From the corner of her eye she caught the young man, the one in the cap, again. Where had he gone? And why was he now watching them with such interest?

"Sister?" Bimmy's curls jangled as her head shifted back and forth.

"Sister!" Cypher's glance darted around backstage, the implication of Audie's message finally sinking in.

Houdini's head tilted back, as if watching a bird escape from his silk top hat. "Speak plainly. This is giving me a migraine."

Cypher leaned in. Audie could barely hear what he was saying. "She went to your dressing room. As planned."

"We saw her," Audie added. Bimmy nodded agreement, curls bouncing with wild abandon.

The scraggly young man in the cap now moved stealthily and intently toward that set of stairs in the back. Why was he being so secretive? Perhaps he had seen Theo. Perhaps he was involved in her absence. Audie made a note to pursue this further.

"It's rather public here," she pointed out. "Difficult for frank conversations."

Houdini followed her gaze, then did a double take as if only then noticing the laboring hordes. Nodded. "Come." He spun on his heel and led them to a door, adorned with a gold star, under which were emblazoned the words HARRY HOUDINI. He turned the door-knob. "We can speak freely in here."

Audie took Bimmy's hand as together they passed into the dressing room of arguably the most famous man in the entire world.

Each wall was plastered with placards shouting out amazing feats: HOUDINI: HANDCUFF KING. HOUDINI: THE JAIL BREAKER. HOUDINI: KING OF CARDS. Each poster featured the man himself, in chains or handcuffs or being lowered into some contraption from which he must escape. Each successive image made Audie's heart race faster.

Bimmy's reaction was not as worshipful. Her circus life had shown her that there was very little magical to magic. But she was polite all the same. Mr. Houdini had, after all, captured the imagination of the world. And no one could deny his escapist skills. Bimmy shuddered to think of the agonies he must endure to break free from those chains and handcuffs and milk cans: dislocated shoulders, broken ribs, slashes, and burns. All for the sake of being called the best.

Cypher was neither admiring nor polite in the midst of Mr. Houdini's gallery of achievements. He was livid. "Where is she?" Cypher lifted up capes and costumes, tossing them to and fro. "She came to you at the appointed time." He had given his word to keep Theodora Quinn safe. She had trusted him. And now she had apparently disappeared! If Houdini had clued Theodora in to Cypher's role, who else had the magician told? Did the man have any idea of how he had compromised everything? Cypher pushed that threatening note from his mind. Surely Theo hadn't been kidnapped right from under his nose.

Houdini shook his head. "She was to come at half past one. But something came up." He indicated Bobby, now sleeping soundly on a fluffy rug. "My dog needed fresh air, if you catch my drift."

Cypher exhaled so forcefully Audie felt as if she might be blown out of the room. "You were not here at the appointed time?" he asked.

Houdini flapped his hand. "I was gone mere minutes. Perhaps ten at the most." It might have been longer; he had stopped to buy a sour pickle from a street urchin. It was nearly as delicious as those his mother used to make. But he didn't see the need in explaining that. Not to someone who was working for *him*.

Audie's hand went to her left ear. "Cypher—"

"Don't move." Cypher's command required complete obedience; even Houdini complied. "Let me examine the room for clues." Cypher shut his eyes, reaching out his hands, palms down. He seemed to be led by his hands, as if they were divining rods, to the far corner of the room. Behind a huge trunk.

"My ear is buzzing like anything," Audie said.

Cypher had had only one experience with the predictive powers of Audie's ear, but one experience was sufficient. "We must stay calm." Outwardly, he was a rock. Inwardly, he was the cream with which Beatrice stuffed her éclairs.

Audie nodded, but her stomach snarled itself into knots like a balky ball of yarn.

"Your ear?" Houdini asked.

"If it's the ear," Bimmy pronounced solemnly, "it's very bad." She said a silent prayer for Theo's safety.

Houdini fell into a leather armchair. "I am completely perplexed by you people." He rubbed his temples. "And profoundly disappointed. You assured me you would keep Theo quiet—" He cut a look at the girls. "I mean, safe." He pounded a fist on his thigh. "Good heavens, man. I open the act in mere days! What am I to do?" Curse that Theodora Quinn for being such a pill about giving him all the information he needed for the illusion. She had insisted on reeling it out in bits and pieces; thought it would be safer that way. And now look where that strategy had gotten them.

Cypher shifted a large vase and stopped. He bent down, reaching for an item on the floor.

"Theo's spectacles!" Audie gasped.

"She's been here." Cypher folded the spectacles with care and placed them in his pocket. "That much we know."

The three Pomegrantos sat in silence. There seemed no good answer to the great magician's question at that moment. Audie stole a glance at Cypher. She had never seen him look so defeated. She rubbed at her ear. Was it losing its powers? After all, it had buzzed around the Great Oberon, too. Maybe there was something about magicians that set it off. Or confused it.

Bimmy chewed at a ragged bit of skin on her thumb, making herself recall every detail of the afternoon, once their own audition had been completed. This mental mapping was something Mama had taught her. It meant the difference between life and death on the high wire, Mama insisted. "Take photographs with your mind, my darling, that's the sure way to avoid mistakes." Clinging to her mother's advice, Bimmy flipped through her mind-photographs of the entire afternoon.

After a few moments, she jolted to her feet. "What did you say?" Then she added, "Sir?"

"What?" Houdini pressed his fingertips to his forehead.

"Please, Mr. Houdini," Bimmy begged. "Repeat what you just said."

Houdini looked over at Cypher, who nodded encouragement. "Well, I said something along the lines of, 'I open the act on Friday night. What am I to do?'"

"'What am I to do?' That's what the Great Oberon said." Bimmy held her arms above her head in a classic prizefighter's pose. "In the lobby of the hotel. Those words exactly."

"You are so right!" Audie remembered it now, too. "And the intonation was much like Mr. Houdini's, was it not?"

Bimmy nodded. She clasped her hands under her chin.

It was Houdini's turn to appear confused, but Cypher quickly caught up to the girls' thinking.

"You are supposing that, among his many other talents, Oberon, or rather our Oberon imposter, may be a mimic. He could have watched you leave the dressing room, slipped in, and greeted Theo, copying your voice." Cypher frowned, deep in thought. "But let us remember, we have no proof of this." This jumping to conclusions was going to be the death of him.

"We did catch him eavesdropping on our conversation," Audie said. "Though we were ever so careful not to say too much."

"Whatever you said"—Houdini morosely stroked Bobby over and over again—"it was clearly too much."

✽ CHAPTER FIFTEEN ✽

One Life Gone?

Slobber sprayed from the dogs' muzzles as they pounded the pavement in hard pursuit. Min had managed to keep inches ahead of them during the chase but was starting to fatigue. There was no reasoning with them; she'd attempted to explain her mission, but the pair spoke an unfamiliar dialect of Dog. And if they spoke Cat, they gave no indication of it.

So on she ran, certain she was about to give up another of her nine lives. Generally, she was philosophical about this fact of being feline. But the thought was now unbearable. Both Punk and Audie needed her! Min scrabbled around a corner, barely dodging the heavy hooves of a draft horse straining to pull a wagon laden with kegs of beer. Her sides heaved with the exertion. She paused in the doorway of a church, desperate to catch her breath.

"Rrroowr!" She tried once again to parley some sense into this pair of beasts. But there was no conversing. No rationalizing.

Canine fangs grazed her right hip. That nip would be exceedingly painful later. Assuming there was a later.

She bounded over a row of trash bins, ducked under an organ grinder's feet, and weaseled around a beat cop tapping a stout stick on his palm. Still, those dogs tracked her. Desperate, she changed course, unaware of the fateful consequences of that particular decision.

The dogs thundered after her.

She'd turned into a blind alley. A dead end. There was no way out. No escape.

Min did not cower. She stood her ground, willing to face what came next. She offered a fervent cat prayer that her seventh life could also be spent with Audie.

Still a good ten feet away, the lead dog lunged, teeth bared, snarling. Showers of saliva drenched Min's fur.

This was it. She tensed.

The airborne dog, having made a serious miscalculation, smacked headfirst into the brick wall at Min's back. The second dog hesitated, confused by its partner's howling.

Min hissed, claws unsheathed, resolve renewed. She would not go down without a fight.

The second dog hesitated further.

A grating noise caught Min's ear.

"Here, puss!" A girl waved an arm out an open window directly above her. "Here!"

Both dogs were momentarily distracted by the voice and the arm. It was Min's final chance. Her only chance.

With every remaining ounce of strength, the sleek feline launched herself up, up, up.

And she fell down, down, down.

Until a pair of hands caught her, and whisked her in through the open window.

Min found herself face-to-face with a friendly pair of hazel eyes.

CHAPTER SIXTEEN

Will the Lost Be Found?

"*Do you think Oberon kidnapped Theo?*" *Audie asked Cypher. She,* unfortunately, knew a thing or two about kidnapping.

"Remember." Cypher patted the spectacles in his pocket thoughtfully. "No jumping to conclusions."

"Kidnapped!" Bimmy wiped at her eyes. "Oh, that would be horrible!"

"Ladies, ladies." Mr. Houdini waved his hands like a symphony conductor. "Let's calm down." He picked up a brass bell sitting on the table at his elbow and rang it three times. Bobby licked his chops. He knew that bell meant tea. Which meant treats.

From nowhere, it seemed, an older man appeared. "Yes, my lord?"

"Tea for—" Houdini did a quick head count. "Tea for four, Winston, if you please."

"Very good, sir." The valet disappeared into a side room.

"Where did he come from?" Bimmy whispered to Audie. "I didn't see him when Mr. Houdini arrived, did you?"

"Maybe he lives here." The moment Audie said the words she

realized how ridiculous they were. No one lived at the Hippodrome. Except the animals.

"This is not the time for tea." Audie began pacing the room. "I think we should search the theater. Leave no stone unturned." The misadventure in the nation's capital was recent enough that she remembered too well the ill-treatment of the president's kidnapped niece. Audie was loath to think the same fate might have befallen Theo.

"Not much point in that." Mr. Houdini formed a tent with his fingers. "The villains would've whisked her away as quickly as possible."

"We have no proof that there are villains." Cypher sounded exasperated.

"You only say that because of your inexperience with theater folks." Houdini waggled his finger at Cypher. "There are some very unscrupulous types. Take that fellow in the Midwest who calls himself Boudini, the Handcuff King. And the phony in—"

"Theo may be missing," Cypher clarified. "But we have no proof that she's kidnapped." He put the full force of authority in his voice.

"And don't get me started on the stagehands." Houdini's rant continued unabated.

His words chilled Audie. Stagehands! "I saw someone," she began. "Hanging around backstage." She was instantly sorry she'd said the words. Her ear hadn't even been buzzing.

"There are always hangers-on," Houdini answered with a dismissive wave. "As if some of my skill might rub off on them."

"When was this?" Cypher edged away from Bobby, who was sniffing at his shoe.

Audie pondered Mr. Houdini's words. That must've been it. The poor young man—and he did look poor, in that ragged attire—was no doubt in hopes of learning one or two of the famous magician's secrets. Hadn't Cypher cautioned her time and again about jumping to conclusions?

"Oh, what a lovely tea!" Audie exclaimed, deftly changing the topic. Her feint worked with Houdini but not with Cypher, who made a mental note to do some background checks. Especially on those backstage hangers-on.

Winston carried a large tray with a cheery red teapot and four cups and saucers. Bobby's nose took inventory. He had no interest in the cucumber sandwiches, but he did love frosted tea cakes. He nudged his master's leg and when that did not produce the desired result, he posed in front of the girls. Children were rarely able to resist his big brown eyes. Bobby wagged his tail, increasing his charm.

The cups were poured and plates filled. If one had stumbled upon the scene, one would have thought to have interrupted a genial gathering of friends. But the four sipped and nibbled in silence.

Houdini's thoughts were full of headlines: *The Great Magician Fails to Vanish an Elephant.* He shuddered to think of what would happen to his reputation. Even though the tea cakes were his favorite—chocolate with raspberry filling—worry turned their flavor to sawdust.

Cypher's concerns teetered back and forth, as if on a scale. On one side were his worries about Theo. How had she disappeared right from under his nose? And if he had failed to keep her safe, was he also likely to fail in protecting Audie and Bimmy? The other side tipped to the practical: Botching this job would mean a discharge from the Pinkerton Detective Agency.

Bimmy's mental gymnastics tumbled between Theo's disappearance and the recent actions of her dearest friend, which were leading Bimmy to believe that Audie was keeping something from her. Since the secret of the library at the School for Wayward Girls had been revealed—Miss Maisie had insisted on calling it the Punishment Room, thus all the girls save Audie had avoided it like the plague—Audie had pledged to play the straight arrow with Bimmy at all times. But Bimmy had been at a loss to explain the flurry of letters she'd seen exchanged prior to departing Miss Maisie's. With whom had Audie been corresponding? And about what?

Audie's thoughts were similar to those of the others sipping tea. Were magicians such a jealous lot that one would deprive Mr. Houdini of his once-in-a-lifetime chance? What could drive someone to such an act of perfidy? She puzzled, too, over Theo's disappearance happening so quickly and under so many noses. Audie again wrestled with whether to mention the scraggly lad she'd seen earlier, deciding to hold off for now. No jumping to conclusions, as Cypher said. On top of everything else, Audie had a letter that she needed to answer, one that would require privacy, a difficult commodity when bunking with one's dearest chum.

The dressing room was so quiet one could have heard fleas jumping through Bobby's fur, had he been so afflicted.

Winston cleared his throat. "May I pour more tea?" He held up the cheery pot.

"No thank—" Audie was interrupted by a knock at the door. Winston opened it.

"Did I leave my spectacles in here?" Theo asked. "I can't seem to find them anywhere."

The girls flew to her. "We've been so worried!" Audie exclaimed.

Bimmy wiped away a tear.

"Rather good to see you." Cypher's calm demeanor belied his immense relief. Of course, this meant his job was no longer in jeopardy. But far more important, Theo appeared unharmed.

"Where have you been?" Houdini stood, checking his pocket watch as he strode across the room. "The run-through is in less than an hour."

Theo shook her head, with a chuckle. "You are mistaken. Why we've loads of ti—" She glanced at her own watch, pinned to her bodice. "Oh, dear." Her forehead wrinkled. "Did I fall asleep?" she murmured. "I must have. I feel so refreshed."

"So you don't know what you've been doing for this past hour or more?" Audie said.

Theo pressed her fingers to her lips, giving the impression of one casting about for thought. "I recall studying the pulleys and levers backstage. And I recall knocking on the dressing room door." She tugged on the string knotted around her left index finger as if it might improve her memory.

Cypher handed her the spectacles, grave concern etched on his face. "Do you recall greeting Mr. Houdini here in this room, after you knocked?"

Theo placed her spectacles on her face and then accepted tea from Winston, who had conjured up a fifth cup from somewhere.

"Lovely; thanks." She sipped. "I'm sorry to be so fuzzy." Her cup clinked against the saucer. "It's as if I've taken a huge eraser to my memory. There's nothing here"—she tapped on her head—"except finding myself backstage without my spectacles and feeling that I'd left them in here."

"Could you have fainted?" Audie wondered aloud. "That happened to me once when I had forgotten to eat."

"I do often forget to eat when I'm busy at work on an experiment," Theo said. "But I had a lovely bowl of oatmeal this morning so I don't think I fainted from hunger." At the mention of hunger, however, she reached for a tea cake, dispatching it in two bites.

"And you feel refreshed?" Bimmy asked.

"With no memory." Houdini returned to his chair, then glanced over at Bimmy. "I suspect you and I are thinking similar thoughts."

Bimmy flushed to be included in the conversation this way. "Hypnotism?" she posited.

Houdini pointed his finger at her. "Bingo," he said. "It is the only reasonable explanation."

Audie was fascinated. She'd never met anyone who'd been hypnotized before! "Who on earth did this to you?"

"May I remind us all once again not to jump to conclusions?" Cypher sighed.

"Every magician has dabbled in that art," Houdini said.

"So, a theater bill full of magicians and other such types means we are faced with many suspects." Audie brushed cake crumbs from her lap. "Therefore it is imperative that we find a motive!" She was so pleased she had recently reread Mr. Houdini's own book on the criminal element.

"A motive's not difficult to deduce." Mr. Houdini handed his cup and saucer to Winston. "In fact, it's obvious. Professional jealousy. Someone wants me to fail at my illusion. And they've somehow connected Theo with the act."

"But how?" Cypher wondered aloud. "Your meetings have been in secret, have they not?"

"Absolutely." Houdini patted his lap and Bobby hopped up. The terrier nosed at the magician's pockets to no avail.

"And we've been so careful here not to give anything away." Audie stopped. "Oh, dear. What would people think of you being in Mr. Houdini's dressing room now?"

A stunned look flashed across Cypher's face.

As she had on the train, Bimmy once again came to the rescue. "We'll say the Pomegrantos requested an audience with Mr. Houdini to bring him greetings from the people of España."

"Bees and bonnets," Audie exclaimed with admiration. "You're good!"

"I agree." Mr. Houdini scratched Bobby under the chin. "This meeting is easily explained."

"Meeting!" Theo glumly held up her be-stringed right pinkie. "You came to my lodgings that day."

Houdini appeared flustered. "Well, I was forced to. You never answered my correspondence," he snapped.

"She's a busy scientist!" Audie came to Theo's defense.

Theo fiddled with the pinkie string. "My landlord, Mr. Billy Bottle, is not the most upright of fellows. I'm afraid if he saw a chance to make some money, he would leap at it. He would probably feel it was his right, what with my rent in arrears."

"So you think someone bribed him in an effort to find the connection between you and Mr. Houdini?" Cypher asked.

"I wouldn't put it past him," Theo answered. "He cheats at cards," she offered. "I should know. I've never beat him in a game of gin rummy."

Cypher made a mental note. Was Mr. Billy Bottle a possible card shark? What else might Theo's landlord be hiding about his past?

"Well," Audie jumped in enthusiastically. "Have you noticed any strangers paying a visit to Mr. Bottle lately?" She breathlessly awaited Theo's reply.

"I'm sorry." Theo reached for a cucumber sandwich, unaware of the one slice of cucumber sliding onto her lap. Bobby was quick to leap across the room to rescue the errant vegetable. "I spend most of my days with my books. Except, as I said, for the odd game of gin or cribbage."

Houdini consulted his pocket watch. "We will have to leave you detectives to your work."

Audie sat up taller in her chair, thrilled at being called a detective.

"Miss Quinn and I have a run-through to discuss." Houdini stood and indicated for Winston to usher everyone else out of the dressing room.

"We will get right to work," Cypher assured the world-famous magician.

But Houdini appeared not to hear this remark. He and Theo were already deep in discussion, heads nearly touching.

Audie was the last one out of the dressing room. "Thank you for the tea," she said to Winston.

The valet nodded and closed the door to further conversation.

"I want you two to go back to the hotel," Cypher instructed. "And stay there."

"But surely there's something we can do," Audie said.

"Yes, there is." Cypher put his hands on her shoulders. "Go back to the hotel and stay put. Do not leave. Do not speak with anyone. Especially not strangers."

"But how can we help if we're at the hotel?" Audie asked.

"Trust me," said Cypher. "That will be a huge help." He pulled some money from his pocket for cab fare. "I should be back in time to take you to dinner. If I'm not, order something from room service." With that he turned and disappeared into the cool dark of the backstage.

Audie and Bimmy stepped out onto Sixth Avenue. Bimmy expertly flagged down a cab. The girls climbed aboard and gave the address of the Evelyn Hotel.

"What do you think Cypher is going to do?" Bimmy settled back in the seat.

"I don't know. More undercover work, I imagine." Audie fussed with the ribbons on her tunic. They'd all been so distracted by Theo's disappearance, they hadn't changed back into their street clothes. "Bees and bonnets!" Audie smothered a giggle. "I do hope he's changed out of his costume." Both girls laughed to imagine Cypher engaged in covert activities while attired in red tights.

"Where do you think he'll start?" Bimmy asked. "Interviews with the stagehands?"

"Speaking of that." Audie chewed her lip. "Did you happen to notice a ragged-looking young man backstage? Battered hat? Lumpy pockets?"

"I didn't. What about him?"

Audie recalled Cypher's warning about not jumping to conclusions. "Nothing. Yet," she said.

The driver pulled up in front of the Evelyn. The girls thanked him. He tipped his hat.

Audie dawdled a bit as she followed Bimmy to the lobby. She knew there would be a letter awaiting her, a letter she did not want Bimmy to see. Casually, she removed a white glove from her pocket, dropping it behind the enormous Boston fern by the reception desk.

Upstairs, she unlocked the door to room 513 and then made a big show of patting her coat. "Oh, dear," she exclaimed. "I'm missing a glove. I wonder if it fell out downstairs."

Bimmy had been shrugging out of her own coat but immediately tugged it back on. "We'll go look."

"You get comfy!" Audie insisted. "I'll be back before you know it." She swiftly closed the door to forestall any protestations. At the end of the hall, the elevator opened and she hurried inside, joining a man with a very large nose. It was such an unforgettable nose above such a scrubby moustache that Audie instantly placed the man. He'd been in the lobby when Theo Quinn had introduced herself.

"Good afternoon," she said, once again ignoring Cypher's admonition about speaking to strangers.

"It is a good afternoon at that." The man folded a small piece of paper and tucked it into his vest pocket. When the elevator landed at the lobby, he strode ahead of her, whistling with enthusiasm and cheer.

Audie gathered her mail, and her glove, but was preoccupied by a flurry of questions as she rode the clanking elevator up to the fifth floor. Who was that man? What was his business here? And why was he whistling?

And more important, how was she going to read and reply to the letter in her pocket without attracting Bimmy's attention?

CHAPTER SEVENTEEN

Pachyderms and Pickles

"That's going to be sore," the girl pronounced after washing the place where the dog had nipped Min's flank. The girl set out a very small saucer of cream. Then she left Min to further nurse her wounds and her pride.

Had she been asked, Min's rescuer could not have explained why she had opened the window and encouraged the cat. It wasn't as if anyone ever lent her a hand. Perhaps she'd helped because she was still feeling giddy over the whole dime she'd bullied from those two greenhorns the other day. Daisy hadn't seen a dime in weeks. Months. She was generally lucky to get a penny for a pair of pickles.

"Don't even think of keeping that cat," Daisy's mother declared. The older woman reeked of dill and the tang of vinegar and was preoccupied with great kettles that gave off enough steam to turn the apartment into a sauna. "We can barely feed ourselves."

"I know. I know." Daisy opened the window again. Looked out. The dogs were nowhere to be seen. "It won't stay." Of that she was sure, though Daisy would be hard-pressed to explain from whence her certainty derived.

Min *merrow*ed her agreement with Daisy's remark; she had no intention of staying. But she did inspect the small apartment, which was a flurry of activity—and nearly as crowded as had been the train station earlier. Min's tour of the domicile required very little time; how long does it take a clever cat, even one with a sore hind leg, to explore three tiny rooms? But every step through that bedroom, parlor, and kitchen required care to stay out of the way of many pairs of feet.

One half of the sole table in the parlor was heaped with knobby green objects, which Daisy wrapped in bits of waxed paper and stuffed into a canvas sack. Another handful of humans sat at the far side of the table, rolling potent dried leaves into long sticks. These, Min discerned, were called *cigars*. The green things had an odd name that she couldn't quite translate into Cat; it sounded like *pickle*, but surely not even humans used such a ridiculous-sounding word.

Min was grateful for her rescue and for the dish of cream, no matter how meager. She hinted for a taste of something else, but nothing else was offered. The humans in this place had an amazing capacity for working hard without taking sustenance. In contrast, the humans at Miss Maisie's did very little but ate three times a day, sometimes more if you counted the French girl's amuse-bouches, little afternoon snacks that Min was happy to help consume.

Seeing that there would be no further nourishment, Min meowed her thanks to Daisy for the open window at just the right moment and then was out that very window again, working her way to the pavement, tracking the now scant scent of Punk. Those dratted dogs had chased her a dreadfully long distance.

Though she dodged plenty of people and carts and wagons and noisy automobiles, Min thankfully encountered no more unfriendly canines on her trek. An old mutt nosing around a set of ash cans gave her rather good directions to the general area. And a sharp-looking Dalmatian at a fire station led her the rest of the way, right up to the back door of an enormous building called the Hippodrome. Dalmatians are always glad to go the extra mile.

Min had arrived at feeding time. Workers wheeled barrows loaded with assorted fruits and vegetables through a large door. Min's instinct was to follow the food. As always, those instincts were spot-on. She followed the worker with the largest barrow—an entire watermelon teetered on top of an enormous heap of foodstuffs—and he led her into the cold, dark innards of the building. She caught a whiff of the Dobermans; thankfully, that was the only sign of them. She padded confidently past pacing tigers—greeting them with due deference—and bears and monkeys and even an odd barking creature that smelled like the sea, until she found the cage she sought. Though he was housed next to some larger, older creatures of his own kind, Punk was no happier. In fact, if it could be possible, he was even more downcast than when Min had last seen him.

"Merrrow?" Min asked permission to enter the cage.

Punk's reply was barely audible. His large ears drooped, but he reached for Min with that long appendage, wrapping it around her middle, drawing her close.

"He misses his mother." This gentle voice came from a gray mountain in the cage next door.

"They took him too young," another voice further explained.

Min pondered this. While she herself had never experienced motherhood, she could remember back to her kitten days and the sweet weeks with her own mum. Despite having to compete for milk with too many greedy brothers, those had been tender times. And, as she had with all her litter, her mother had let Min stay until she was ready to go off on her own. Min shivered to think what kind of cat she might have become had she been taken from her mother, and taken too young. No doubt the worst kind: a scaredy-cat.

Several hours passed as Min did her best to comfort Punk. When he finally drifted off to sleep, she remained, hidden from human eyes in the dark of the cell. While he slept, the other creatures of his kind talked about their lives. Poor Punk had little to look forward to—hours of being chained to a wall, thrashings, tricks that required un-elephant-like contortions.

"He's too frail," the largest of the creatures, named Jennie, explained. "He won't last."

"There must be something we can do," Min said.

Jennie raised her own shackled foot, skin scarred around the metal. "There's no escape."

The resignation in Jennie's voice was more chilling than an ice bath. Min would not accept this for Punk. What was it Audie liked to say? If it's not splendid, it's not the end?

"My friend can save him," Min declared, bristling with confidence.

"But how?" Jennie asked.

"I don't know," Min answered truthfully. "All I know is that she can."

Her words of hope shed powerful light in that dark and dreary place.

CHAPTER EIGHTEEN

You Are Getting Sleepy

He caught her outside the theater. "Good evening," he said, twirling the moustache under his large nose like a silent-screen villain.

Surprised to see the man, Theo adjusted her spectacles. It had been a long two days and she was eager to get to her rooms. There was a wrinkle in the illusion that needed ironing out before she would connect with her pillow that night.

"Good evening," she answered, ever polite no matter how weary.

"You're working late," the man noted, checking the time on his pocket watch.

"Oh, you know what they say." She lifted her hem to step off the curb. "No rest for the wicked." For some reason, she could not take her gaze from the pocket watch, now swaying to and fro.

"That's a lovely watch," she said. After five fros, her voice changed. It was dull, automatic. "I am at your command," she said.

The man chuckled. Oh, this was rich. This was sweet! The earlier afternoon session had been successful. She really was in his power.

"You remember what you are to do?" he asked, barely able to control his joy as he anticipated the answer.

"I am to stop the elephant from vanishing," she said. "I am to ruin Houdini."

The watch stopped its swinging. It was returned to the man's vest pocket. "Very good." He snapped his fingers. "You're working late," he said.

"Oh, you know what they say." Theo stepped off the curb. "No rest for the wicked." She crossed Sixth Avenue, eager to get home, feeling surprisingly refreshed, despite the long and stress-filled day.

CHAPTER NINETEEN

An Unwanted Visitor

"You were up early this morning," Bimmy said.

"Up early?" Audie tried to sound nonchalant as she buttoned up her boots.

Bimmy reached for her own button hook. "I heard you step out."

"I wanted to make sure that postcard to the triplets went out in the first mail." Even though it was for Bimmy's benefit, Audie did so dislike misleading her friend. Though her statement was partially true, she could not bear the glimmer of suspicion in Bimmy's eyes.

To Audie's great luck, Cypher's knock on the door was sufficient distraction. He had come to take them to breakfast and then on to the theater for rehearsals. The three had the elevator to themselves so Audie could not resist asking what he had learned.

Cypher had slept well so he didn't see the harm in answering Audie's question. "Well, our Oberon is really a man by the name of Wylie Wurme, also a magician and illusionist, but there is no evidence of Wurme ever performing Oberon's signature act." Cypher's left eyebrow arched. "Seems his essential equipment goes missing in some way before each show."

"So it wasn't really stolen!" Audie exclaimed.

They had clunked to a stop on the ground floor and the doors rattled open. Cypher's forefinger went to his lips. "Seems so," was all he said as they stepped into the lobby.

The fourth chair at their table in the nearby café remained empty all through breakfast.

"Perhaps Theo forgot she was to join us?" Bimmy suggested, crunching the last bite of bacon on her plate. She wiggled her fingers. "Maybe she ran out of string."

"Or maybe she was working late at the theater." Audie sprinkled a little more brown sugar on her oatmeal. "And overslept."

"I think it's likely the latter," Cypher said. "According to Mr. Houdini, there were still a lot of loose ends to tie up." He took note of the time and then encouraged the girls to finish up. "I don't relish paying the five-dollar late fine," he told them as he paid the check.

As minor acts on the bill, they did not have grand dressing rooms of their own. Cypher shared one with the English acrobats, a tap dancer, and Herring's trainer, as well as some of the other men and boys. The women's shared dressing room was on the second floor, up a rickety, narrow stairway. Audie and Bimmy politely stopped at the bottom, allowing the opera diva to go ahead of them.

"*Buongiorno.*" The diva acknowledged them with a dip of her head.

"*Buenos dios.*" Bimmy winked at Audie. "That's how we say good morning in our native country."

"Buenos dios," Audie echoed, unaware she was mimicking an inaccurate phrase.

The opera diva was a solid woman and it took some time for her to progress up the stairs. As Audie waited her turn to ascend to the dressing room, she glanced around backstage. Ten in the morning was the theater's witching hour, when everything came to life. Some stagehands were testing the ropes, some moving props, and one of the costumers was mending a tear in the thick velvet stage cushion.

A flash of fur low to the ground caught Audie's attention. Chocolate-striped! Min!

Audie stopped herself from calling aloud. Surely a cat would not be a welcome backstage addition. If Bert knew, he would be likely to throw her out. But how did Min get there? And where was she headed?

"I'll be right back." Audie dashed after her cat, following her down the stairs. Min's pace picked up and so did Audie's. The smell was powerful in this space deep below the grand stage: Old hay and animal dung made Audie's eyes water. But she ran on, after Min.

When she saw Min slip between some heavy metal bars, she couldn't help crying out. "Min! Take care." Audie ran even faster, grasping the cold bars in her hands as she caught up with her cat.

There was Min, cradled in a baby elephant's trunk. Though Audie's ears were not buzzing, her heart began to pound. Elephants were dangerous! She herself was an orphan all because of these great beasts. She tried to call to Min, but all the saliva had gone from her mouth. Her tongue clicked against dry teeth. She cleared her throat and tried again. "Here, Min. Here, puss." She patted her leg for Min to come to her.

But Min did not. She blinked, her golden eyes shining like flashlights into Audie's heart. Audie's grip on the bars relaxed. She watched Min nimbly climb up the elephant's trunk to a flat spot near the back of its head. Then Min began bathing the elephant, as if it were a kitten, giving special care to the tops of its boat-sail ears.

This was a baby elephant, Audie could see that. An orphan, no doubt; who better than Audie to know the pain of that situation? "What's your name, little fellow?" she asked, her heart softening. Audie glanced around and noticed a small placard on the wall near the cage. "Baby? Is that you?"

The elephant made a snuffling noise, raising its trunk slightly, as if confirming Audie's guess. As her eyes grew accustomed to the dark, Audie could see that the young creature was chained to the wall. Her heart sank further when she saw the raw spots on its foreleg, the one ensnared in some kind of manacle.

Without words, Audie and Min and Baby remained in one another's company for a good while, rehearsals and costumes and magicians completely forgotten.

* * *

Jamie shifted his cap back on his head, considering this intruder.

Maybe Helmut had tumbled to Jamie's activities. Sent this girl as a spy. What *else* could she be up to? Wasn't she a juggler, along with that Persian man? They must be some kind of team; they wore matching garish costumes. You'd never catch Jamie in laces and tights like that!

He turned back to the matter at hand. The girl.

Jamie shifted slightly in the dark recess, silent as midnight, but still the girl stopped. Turned. He ducked and nearly tripped over something low to the ground. Something alive. He shuddered, remembering the rat-infested wards at the orphanage. When he caught the stripes on the creature's back, he exhaled in relief. It was only a cat! A cat that circled his legs before slipping fearlessly through the bars into Baby's cage. What on earth? Curiosity overcame common sense, and he stepped out of the shadows.

"They're friends." The girl uttered the words as if in prayer. "Good friends." She turned toward Jamie, her face ghostly in the dim light.

Jamie was so drawn to the scene that he was now standing at the girl's shoulder.

"Are you Baby's keeper?" the girl asked.

Jamie nodded. "Assistant," he clarified.

The girl's hand trembled as she pointed to the bull hook hanging on the wall. "Do you use that?"

"Never."

She nodded. "I've read about them. In *Harmsworth Natural History* and other books." She blushed, fearing she sounded quite the snob. "They're social creatures, as well you know."

Jamie grunted. He knew no such thing. Wasn't even sure what "social" meant.

"Do you know they can live for seventy or eighty years?" she asked. "Well, more like forty in captivity."

Jamie looked over at Baby. How old was he? Not even a year? He got sick at his stomach thinking of that sweet creature living another forty or fifty years under Helmut's "care." "That so?"

She nodded. "And it's horrible what we do to them."

Jamie stiffened. He had done his best to show Baby nothing but kindness. "I take good care of this one, I do."

"Oh, I have no doubt about that." The girl slipped two volumes from the costume bag she carried and offered them to Jamie.

He glanced at the titles. *Harmsworth Natural History. Animal Kingdom, Volume 1,* it said. Volume one! How many books *were* there about animals? About elephants? "Might I borrow these?" Jamie asked.

"Of course." The slim young thing held out her hand. "Audacity Jones. Audie to my friends."

"Pleased to meet you, miss." He shook, tipped his cap. "Jamie Doolan."

Audacity cocked her head, as if listening for something. A long moment passed. It felt to Jamie as if his worth had been weighed and measured. "I can't bear to think of Baby trapped here forever," she said. "Neither can Min." She nodded her head toward the cage.

"Is that your cat, then?" Jamie stuffed the books in his pocket. "Best to keep her out of Bert's sight. He doesn't like cats. Says they make him sneeze."

"She's very clever," Audacity said. "She'll stay out of Bert's way."

Jamie hadn't much experience with cats. But this one did appear to have good sense. And Baby had taken to her, hadn't he? "That's a sight that warms my heart," he added, watching cat and elephant together.

"Doolan!" A harsh voice shredded the quiet. "Where are you?"

Min jumped down, having completed Baby's toilette.

"You two best be going," Jamie urged. He reached for a pitchfork, so Helmut would find him working. "My boss wouldn't like you taking up with Baby." He flipped dirty straw into a wheelbarrow.

The shouting grew louder and closer.

"There's a way out, over there," Jamie said. "Hurry."

"We're going." Audacity patted the bars of Baby's cage. "But we'll be back."

"*Mer-row,*" added the cat.

CHAPTER TWENTY

If It's Not Splendid

It was Lilac's day to be head of the Order of Percy, so it was she who answered the door to the telegram delivery boy who insisted he must surrender his missive directly to Miss Maisie's hand. But Lilac took him into the kitchen where Beatrice served him hot chocolate and fresh croissants, and he soon forgot about telegrams altogether.

"Won't you have another?" Lilac offered. "Four croissants is hardly enough for a strapping young lad such as yourself."

"I think I have room," the delivery boy answered with chocolate-stained lips. Lilac delivered the fifth pastry on a small sterling tray. "Let me get *this* out of the way." She slid the telegram into her pocket. The boy—in a chocolate-and-butter stupor—did not even notice.

After reading the message, Lilac set about finding her sisters. Violet was teaching the littlest Waywards to ride the School's one bicycle. Lavender was leading interpretive dance sessions in the parlor. "Important meeting," she whispered in her sisters' ears. "Ten minutes."

When the meeting was convened in their hiding spot, Lilac shared the telegram.

"Oh, dear," Lavender sniffled, threatening to burst into a full-blown sobbing episode. "How on earth could we possibly help?"

"Tears are not going to solve anything." Envisioning Audie's own response, Violet squeezed her sister's hand firmly. "Audie left us in charge. And if she thinks we're capable of assisting with her scheme, we cannot disappoint." To remind her sisters of all they owed Audie, she merely held up a fabric fragment of Audie's old stuffed giraffe.

Lavender hiccupped softly, putting an end to any waterworks. "But hiding an elephant?" Her blue eyes grew wide. "How on earth could we do that?"

Lilac chewed her lip, concentrating. "We need someplace big," she said.

"And free," added Lavender. "We don't have any money."

Violet nodded. "These are mighty obstacles." Her fingers stroked the tiny bit of Percy's ear.

The triplets sat quietly, racking their brains for an idea.

"You know." Lilac hesitated. Should she reveal what she'd heard in the still of the night? It might offer a solution to the problem at hand. Yet it was Divinity's secret. Lilac weighed the pros and cons and arrived at a decision. "Divinity said something very odd in her sleep." After drawing a deep breath, she confided all in her sisters.

"Farm?" Violet's ears perked up. "But that's the perfect solution!"

"She'd never agree." Lavender's eyes glistened. "It's hopeless."

For a moment, Violet, too, nearly succumbed to doubt. Then an image of their initiation ceremony flashed in her mind. "What does Audie always say?"

The girls knew the words so well, they did not need to say them aloud.

Violet clapped her hands together, once. "All right, then. We need to get to work."

CHAPTER TWENTY-ONE

Plenty of Dr. Leo's Breathene

Bert's head ached from sneezing. His eyes itched. And now worry was eating a hole clean through his stomach. Why hadn't he taken his mother's advice and become a fireman? There was a nice quiet life, to be sure.

So far, with tomorrow's big show looming, he had a trained seal that required quarts of fresh herring, which were apparently in short supply in New York City; a set of jugglers who really couldn't juggle; and an usher that could not hand out programs. Bert wiped his brow with a red bandana. At least, the headline act was sound. Mr. Houdini would never let him down, though it exasperated Bert that everything surrounding this new illusion was so mysterious-like. Only certain stagehands were being let in on certain bits. None of it was to his liking, but Bert understood the need for secrecy. Magicians tended to be overly protective of new acts; less chance for some competitor to poach it.

Bert dosed himself with Dr. Leo's Breathene, and then took a bite of the lunch his wife had prepared. Liverwurst on rye. Not ideal for a nervous stomach, but she meant well. He swallowed, then took a swig of the carbonated water at his elbow. Belched. If he survived the next few days, he would buy some acreage in New Jersey. Build a small house with a picket fence. Give piano lessons. He took another swig of the carbonated water.

He also had to survive the meeting with the Hippodrome's owners, set to start in five minutes. Bert polished off his sandwich, then headed to the Shubert brothers' office. The first item on the agenda was the balky "usher." That poor baby elephant. Bert could barely stomach being around Helmut. All the rough talk about power and submission. It certainly wasn't having a successful impact on Baby. No matter what Helmut did, the creature could not seem to grasp the idea of using its trunk to hand out programs to patrons. Bert felt it was a lost cause.

"Just have him stand outside the theater," he suggested at the meeting. "People love baby animals. They won't care that he can't hand out programs."

"He can learn." Helmut glared at Bert. "He *will* learn."

Bert felt Helmut would have used the whip on *him* had he been given the chance.

The brother owners conferred and then decided to give Helmut another chance. "It's the perfect gambit to complement Houdini's illusion," Mr. J. J. Shubert, the plumper of the two, said.

"Perfect," Helmut echoed.

Bert changed the subject. "This Oberon keeps pestering to audition," he said. "Says he has a boffo levitation gimmick."

Mr. Lee Shubert flicked his hand about. "Put him off." He sniffed. "Those suckers only care about Houdini, not Algernon."

"Oberon," Bert corrected quietly.

"So it's all a go for the Vanishing Elephant illusion?" Mr. J. J. Shubert asked.

Bert caught a sneeze in his red bandana. "Of course. Of course." He coughed out a laugh. "Does Houdini ever disappoint?"

"There's always a first time," said Mr. J. J. Shubert.

"You're not catching cold, eh, Bert?" asked Mr. Lee Shubert.

"No cold," Bert said to the first Mr. Shubert. "And no disappointment," he said to the second, with far more confidence than he felt. "Houdini's Vanishing Elephant illusion is going to be the talk of the town."

The owners nodded, satisfied. "Talk of the town is fine," one said, "but it's filled seats we're after." With this pronouncement, Mr. Lee Shubert stood, signaling the end of the meeting. Mr. J. J. Shubert followed his brother to the door.

Forcing a smile as he saw the brothers out, Bert spoke reassuringly. "Oh, we'll fill seats all right." And he hoped with all his might that his words would come true.

CHAPTER TWENTY-TWO

Roll Out the Barrels

"You're not still fretting over dropping the balls at rehearsal, are you, chum?" Bimmy asked. Audie had been uncharacteristically quiet on the stroll back to the hotel. She pulled Audie out of the path of a businessman briskly swinging a large valise as he strode past.

"It's not that." Audie was on the verge of confessing one of her secrets to Bimmy, but she bit back the words. It was one thing to assume the risk for herself; she could not involve her sweet friend. "I was merely wondering how everything was going back at Miss Maisie's."

"I'm sure the triplets are managing just fine," Bimmy assured her, now tugging Audie out of the way of a pair of sturdy matrons, both of whom tsk-tsked at the girls as they passed. "I don't think I would ever get used to all the people if I lived here."

"People?" Audie nearly collided with a pram. The nanny pushing it deftly steered around her.

"Your mind really is far away," Bimmy said. "Are you sure there isn't something you'd like to chat about?"

Again, Audie felt the temptation to share. Bimmy had loads and loads of circus experience. And circuses had to transport items of all shapes and sizes. "Oh, sometimes my mind gets taken with the oddest notions." Audie did her best to act as if discussing the most trivial of concerns. She would come at this through the back door. "For example, how on earth does our friend Herring get moved from town to town?"

This was familiar ground to Bimmy. "Well, the big circuses have their own special rail cars, like rolling cages, that the wild cats and such ride in. But a seal like Herring could travel in a smaller cage, even in a baggage car."

Trains were a logical choice. But also very public. How would one hide an elephant, though small, using that mode of transportation? "But, Bimmy, what if the circus was a lesser one? Or what if it were traveling to a town without train service?"

The girls held their noses as they passed a street sweeper at work. Audie did not envy that poor street sweeper. In one quick glance, she counted over a dozen horses carrying cabs and wagons up one side of the street and down the other.

Once they were safely past the odiferous pile of horse droppings, Bimmy removed her fingers from her nose to point. "See those cart horses there?"

Audie followed Bimmy's fingers. "Bees and bonnets! They're huge." Two magnificent creatures, muscles rippling as they worked in unison, steadily pulled a wagon heaped with large barrels labeled MAGIC CITY SOUR PICKLES.

"They're Percherons," Bimmy explained. "Bred to carry large

loads. When we were in the Barley and Bingham Circus, they had a stable of them. Each pair carried a cage on wheels."

Audie studied the horses and the wagon they pulled. The horses appeared to haul the loaded wagon with ease, clip-clopping down the street. "What kind of animals were in that circus?" she asked.

Bimmy squinched up her face, remembering. "The usual. A lion, two tigers. A bear, the cart horses, of course, and some performing horses. A dog act." She tapped her forefinger to her mouth, thinking. "Oh yes. And Pearl."

"Pearl?"

"She was the gentlest creature," Bimmy said. "Her trainer used to let me ride on her back in the big-top parade."

"So Pearl was a horse," Audie guessed.

"No. An elephant." Bimmy gestured with her arms. "One of the biggest I've ever seen."

Audie's heart skittered in her chest. She did her best to reply calmly. "And two horses could pull Pearl's cage?"

"Easily." Bimmy took Audie's arm as they approached the curb. A hansom cab barreled past, not even slowing for the girls or any of the other pedestrians. "It looks safe to cross now," she said.

Audie felt lighthearted as she strolled next to Bimmy the rest of the way to the hotel. Surely there was a wagon master in this city willing to give a baby elephant a ride. She wiggled the toes in her left boot. If necessary, the gold coin in that boot could cover any expenses incurred.

Now all she needed was to find a haven for Baby. It was a daunting task, to be sure. But hadn't that Mr. Henry Ford once said,

"If you think you can do a thing or think you can't do a thing, you're right"? That's why she'd sent the telegram to Miss Maisie's. One never knew where answers might lie.

Audie was choosing to think she could do this thing.

Heartened and inspired, she took Bimmy's hand. "I think this calls for ice cream!" She led the way into a nearby drugstore.

"What are we celebrating?" Not that Bimmy needed a reason to eat ice cream.

Audie thought fast. "A successful mission!"

"It's not over yet," Bimmy reminded her. "Maybe it's bad luck to celebrate too soon."

"Nonsense." Audie hopped up on one of the red stools by the soda fountain. She patted the seat next to her. "Nothing could possibly go wrong now."

CHAPTER TWENTY-THREE

The No-Good
Jamie Doolan

The Shubert brothers frowned. "I thought you could teach any elephant anything," J. J. said.

"Not this one." Helmut banged on the cage bars. "Stupid as they come."

"He looks bright enough," Lee Shubert observed.

"If it were me," Helmut said, "I'd get rid of him."

"We spent fifteen hundred dollars on this creature." The two brothers exchanged glances. "We're not accustomed to throwing away good money," said J. J.

Jamie leaned the pitchfork against the wall and stepped forward. It hurt him something awful to hear Helmut speak ill of Baby that way. "Would you allow me to give it a go?" He tugged nervously at his cap.

Helmut snorted. "You?"

"I have an idea—" Jamie began.

"You are a no-good, worthless Irishman," Helmut interrupted. "Fit only to shovel filthy hay."

"I'm Irish, all right." Jamie stood his ground. "But Baby and I understand each other. Both being orphans and all."

"Get back to work." Helmut grabbed the pitchfork and shoved it at Jamie.

"Hold up there." Mr. J. J. Shubert stepped forward. "What harm is there in giving the lad a chance?"

"No harm at all," said Mr. Lee Shubert, cutting off Helmut's opportunity to respond. He nodded to Jamie. "What is your thought, boy?"

"Do you have a piece of paper I might use?" Jamie asked. "As a substitute for a program?"

Both brothers patted their pockets. "What about this?" J. J. pulled out a letter, unfolding it as he handed it over.

Jamie took it, then let himself into Baby's cage. He slowly unfolded the letter while Baby's trunk agitated back and forth. "This won't hurt you." Jamie's voice was soft and kind. "I won't hurt you." He held the paper out. But Baby backed against the bars at the rear of the cage, uneasy with Helmut there as well as two men he didn't know.

"See?" Helmut said. "Uncooperative."

As if comforting an infant, Jamie began to sing "Hush Ye, My Bairnie."

Baby snuffled, patted Jamie with his trunk.

"I think he likes it," the plumper Shubert said, amazed.

Pat. Snuffle. Pat. Snuffle. Pat. Snuffle. Then with a clumsy rocking motion, Baby moved away from the bars, toward Jamie.

"Take a look at this." Jamie held the piece of paper out again. When Baby tapped it with his trunk, Jamie instantly fed him a sugar cube. "Good boy!" Another tap. Another sugar cube. Soon, Baby was taking the paper from Jamie each time it was held out.

"That's amazing!" Mr. Lee Shubert exclaimed.

"This animal looks perfectly cooperative to me," said his brother.

Jamie glanced at Helmut's face, wincing at the fury he saw there. "It was Helmut who laid the groundwork," he said quickly. "I merely reaped the benefit of his skill."

"Of course, of course." The Shuberts shook Helmut's hand. "Anyone can see that. Well done."

"Come upstairs with us," said Mr. J. J. Shubert. "There is a bonus in this for you."

Without so much as a thank-you to Jamie, Helmut left with the Hippodrome's owners.

"Well, now you'll be their pet." Jamie looked around for a bit of fresh fruit to toss to Baby and found nothing. "Okay. Okay." He patted his pockets. His salary was being quickly devoured by Baby's needs. "I'll be right back."

He tore up the stairs and out the door to the neighborhood pushcart vendor.

"Oh, my favorite *klots*," the vendor said by way of greeting.

"I'm glad to see you, too," Jamie replied, throwing coins at the man in exchange for armfuls of fruits and vegetables. He turned and ran back to the Hippodrome's basement, so preoccupied that he wasn't watching where he was going. He was stopped stone-cold when he crashed into someone.

A female someone.

"Sorry, miss!"

"No harm done." The female someone smoothed her skirts, picking up a rutabaga that had gone flying out of Jamie's pocket. "Are you one of those vegetarians?" The young woman held the vegetable in her hand, wearing a thoughtful expression. "How fascinating."

Jamie counted four strings on various slim and ink-stained fingers while he pondered a reply. Was it possible that eyes could be such a shade of brown? He felt he could look at those eyes every day for the rest of his life and never tire of their color.

He shook his head to clear it. What was happening?

"Uh. Not me," he said. "It's my—it's Baby."

She paused. "Your baby?"

He paused, too. Could he trust her? "Would you like to come meet him?"

"Yes," she answered decisively. "Yes, I would."

She followed him down the steps and into the basement, never making one comment about the odors. He stopped in front of Baby's cage.

A trunk snaked out, feeling around for food.

The young woman laughed, offering up the rutabaga. Baby took it, munching happily. "I've never fed an elephant before," she said. "His skin feels like leather. So soft."

As he fed Baby the rest of the vegetables, Jamie cast about in his brain for words of reply. There were none. It was as if he were a toddler who'd not yet learned to speak.

Again a smile. "Are you part of the show?" she inquired.

"The elephant is," Jamie said. "I'm his assistant." Flustered, he shook his head. "That's not what I mean."

The fabulous creature pushed her spectacles up on her nose. "But I think being an elephant's assistant sounds like a fabulous job. Better than mine."

Jamie found his tongue. "What's yours, then?"

"Juggler." The young woman mimed tossing balls.

Baby tapped her arm.

"I'm sorry, friend," she said. "I don't have anything else for you to eat."

"He's had plenty," Jamie assured her. "Leave her be, you cheeky thing."

"I'll be late for rehearsal." The young woman turned to go, and in that movement, Jamie's heart nearly tore in two.

She paused. "Tell me, are they as intelligent as I've read they are?" A notebook appeared from her skirt pocket. A pencil appeared from elsewhere and was now poised over the paper.

Was she having him on? Jamie snuck an earnest glance at her lovely face, all lit up from the inside. He didn't think so. "Whip smart," he said, now doubly glad he'd read the books the other girl had given him. "And loving. They take care of one another." His voice caught, overwhelmed by his memory of failing Kitty. His precious sister.

She peered over her notebook, catching his dismay. "I have been too nosy. I'm sorry." She sighed. "I can't help it. I am completely overcome with the need to gather knowledge. I know it is most unbecoming, but I can't seem to stop myself. But if you do feel like sharing, I would be glad to listen." She blinked those brown eyes at him.

And that was all it took. A dam broke inside, and all the sad Jamie had held within came flooding out: about Kitty and Baby and Helmut and the plan Audie had concocted.

"I see." A smile as warm as a cozy fire spread across her face. "You're a friend of Audacity's?"

"Well, me and Baby," he said, already regretting his confession. Oh, she'd have a good laugh over this with her friends later: a lowly orphan thinking he could be some kind of hero.

She grabbed Jamie's hand and shook it, sending electric jolts up his arm and directly into his heart. "I'm her friend, too." She leaned close, her peppermint breath whiskering against Jamie's ear. "I'm helping Mr. Houdini to vanish one elephant. Perhaps I can be of assistance in vanishing this one, as well." She put her fingers to her lips. "Don't tell, will you?"

They could drag him through the East River and hang him by his toes from the el tracks; Jamie would never give up this creature's secrets.

"I'd best be going now, miss." Jamie was awobble with some emotion unfamiliar to him but which you, dear reader, would recognize as the first stirrings of true love.

"Soon, the city will be amazed at Harry Houdini, vanishing an elephant." She pressed her hand to his arm. "But you and Audie will be the true magicians, Jamie Doolan. And it will be my great honor to be a part of *your* show." With that, she was gone, leaving Jamie's mouth hanging open wide enough for an elephant parade.

CHAPTER TWENTY-FOUR

A Lovely Cuppa Tea

The dress rehearsal was a complete and utter disaster.

The head grip was all smiles. "Good sign, that," he said. "Nothing left to go wrong tomorrow night."

Oh, how Bert wished these words held truth. In a weak moment, he'd agreed to switch around a few acts. He sneezed. These allergies would be the death of him! Had he been feeling himself, he would have stood up to Mr. Houdini. Why he needed that juggling act to perform before him, Bert had no idea. And then that Oberon had been carrying on something awful about getting on the bill. His audition wasn't half bad. Maybe Bert could find a slot for him. But it would have to wait until after tomorrow night. After the Vanishing Elephant. Bert sneezed again. Three times. His aching head. His itching eyes. His raw red nose.

A cup of tea would make him feel better. This backstage chaos could carry on without him for fifteen minutes, at least.

Bert took himself to his office, unaware that he had missed, by moments, a certain girl juggler who had entered carrying a piece of paper but exited without it. He also could not know that this same girl was at that moment conspiring with the assistant elephant keeper.

While Bert waited for the teakettle to whistle, he rummaged in the top desk drawer, seeking a packet of Digestive Biscuits, but instead finding a note he'd written to himself: *Don't forget M's birthday.* The note was days old. Which meant—he glanced at the wall calendar courtesy of Shaffer's Theater Goods to confirm his suspicion—he had indeed forgotten his wife's birthday. What else could possibly go wrong? He reached for the bottle of milk for his tea. This action brought him face-to-face with a sleek chocolate-striped cat with golden eyes.

"You!" Bert sneezed, reaching for his bottle of Dr. Leo's Breathene. "You're the reason I'm falling apart!" He stamped his foot. "Shoo!" Stamped again. "Scat."

The cat neither shooed nor scatted. She twitched her tail. Once. Twice.

Bert must have dozed off in his chair because the next thing he knew, the kettle was shrilling in his ear. He jolted, then pulled it off the hot plate and poured the steaming water over a spoonful of tea in his Brown Betty teapot. Where had the milk gone? And why had he left that saucer on the floor?

The tea steeped to a lovely caramel hue. Bert drank the entire cup and didn't miss the milk, turning his attention to the stack of papers on his desk. He flipped through invoice after invoice, including one requisition for the use of a wagon and two cart horses, all of which he signed with a flourish. Paperwork and tea completed, Bert felt capable of handling any calamity upstairs, including a fish-deprived seal, an opera diva who refused to follow a seal act, and a troupe of bumbling jugglers. He whistled every step of the way, feeling quite chipper though he couldn't say precisely why.

CHAPTER TWENTY-FIVE

Opening-Night Jitters

"When did you start to feel unwell?" Bimmy examined Audie's face with concern.

"It's likely just opening-night jitters." Audie made her most pitiful expression and pressed her hands to her stomach. "Or maybe I shouldn't have eaten that second sandwich at luncheon." She hated misleading Bimmy in this way, but desperate times called for desperate measures. "You go on down to supper with Cypher. I'll be fit as a fiddle after a little rest." She smiled wanly. "The show must go on!"

Bimmy, already in costume, tugged at the tassels dangling from the hem of her skirt. "I don't want to leave you alone."

As if on cue, Min slipped through the window, landing with a soft thump on the floor.

"I'll be in good hands," Audie said. "Or rather, paws. Go on, now. I'll meet you at the theater."

"If you've still got your sense of humor, I suppose it can't be too serious." Bimmy shrugged into her coat. "But I'll make sure it's a very short meal." She fumbled with the buttons. "Perhaps they could even wrap up my supper and I can bring it here to eat. Keep you company."

Audie squirmed under the bedcovers. How could she have underestimated Bimmy's loyalty and concern? "I think the smell of food might make it worse. An hour's rest and I'll be good as gold."

Bimmy bent to tuck the quilt to Audie's chin. "You're always good as gold," she said, placing a little peck on Audie's forehead. "You rest, then. We'll meet you at the theater." Then she was finally on her way.

Audie counted to one hundred, as slowly as she could force herself. "One, two, three . . ." It was agony. "Eighty-five, eighty-six." She peeled back the quilt. "Ninety-nine. One hundred!" She hopped off the bed and grabbed the buttonhook to do up her boots. Min helped by snagging Audie's coat and dragging it over.

"Thank you, Min." Audie fastened the last few boot buttons and slipped into the proffered garment. "Fingers and paws crossed that everything goes according to plan."

Min bounded out the window, while Audie snuck into the hallway to return an exceedingly important phone call. "Yes, it's all arranged," she said into the receiver. "Saturday it is." That mission accomplished, she ducked down the back stairway. It was imperative that she not be seen.

At street level, she cracked the hotel's rear door, peeking left and right before stepping outside. She adjusted her costume bag over her shoulder, then hurried off to see a man about a wagon, a pair of horses, and a very large container. Had her nerves not been in such a state, Audie would have realized that her exit had been observed. At a respectable pace, her acquired shadow followed, leaving a vinegary trail in her wake.

* * *

"I'm worried about Audie," Bimmy confessed. "In all the years I've known her, I've never seen her unwell."

Cypher poked at the meat loaf in front of him, making a mental note not to order the Blue Plate Special in the future. "I thought you said it was opening-night jitters." He tried a bite of mashed potato with gravy. Barely edible.

"Whichever it is, she shouldn't be alone." Bimmy held on to the chair seat with both hands, legs swinging like pendulums. "I have a mind to go back to the hotel. Right now."

"Stay put." Cypher pointed his fork at her chair. "If she's unwell, she needs rest and quiet." He tilted his head in a sideways nod. "Sometimes even the best of friends need a breather from one another."

Bimmy bit her lip. Had she worn out her welcome with Audie? They had chatted rather late into the night, talking about Houdini and Theo and the Pomegrantos. "I suppose you're right," she said glumly.

Cypher set down his utensils, catching something in Bimmy's eyes that tugged at his well-protected heart. Something he recognized. He cleared his throat. "I planned to go by myself," he began. "But I could use a hand with my after-supper errand." He raised an eyebrow at Bimmy. She did not seem to be taking the bait. "Escorting Miss Theodora Quinn to the theater."

"Oh?" She leaned forward the tiniest bit. "Do you suspect trouble tonight?"

He had her now. Best to play it up. Set the hook. He lowered his voice. "I can't talk here."

Bimmy considered. He could sense her about ready to agree. "Well," she started. "I suppose there is safety in numbers."

Cypher smiled, triumphant. It seemed he knew a thing or two about young ladies, after all.

"As long as we hurry," Bimmy added. "I don't want to keep Audie waiting at the theater, you know."

"Yes." He sighed. "Yes, of course."

* * *

Theo answered at the first knock. "I'm almost ready!" She waved them inside. "Come see my laboratory!"

Her hands darted about like finches—scattering bits of string—as she took them on a quick tour. By the time Theo finished showing off her volumetric pipettes and sample tubes and all the different varieties of flasks—Erlenmeyer, and Florence, and filtering—her face was flushed with joy.

"It's wonderful." Bimmy eyes glowed with interest. She could imagine herself in just such a place. Someday. Not now, but someday.

As if reading her mind, Theo said, "I meant it about the standing invitation." She brushed a stray lock of hair away from her face. "You are welcome to join me at any time."

Bimmy nodded her gratitude. "I don't think I could be a city girl," she said.

"I'm hoping to move out to the country somewhere. Peace and quiet and—" Theo stopped. "It's a big dream, I know. But one must have dreams."

Cypher pulled out his pocket watch and tapped it. "We're running late."

"I'll be only a moment!" Theo turned off this Bunsen burner and stoppered that beaker. She dug her costume bag out from under a mountain of papers. "Ready!"

Cypher took the bag from Theo, struggling with its weight. Had she packed bricks along with her ballet slippers, tunic, and tights? Setting such questions aside, he flagged a cab and they were soon inside. Once they were settled on the smooth leather seats, jostling their way to the theater, Cypher removed a small notepad from his vest pocket. "I've been doing some background work on our Mr. Oberon. Does the name Wylie Wurme ring any bells?"

Theo shook her head. "I don't think so."

"He lived in your boardinghouse at one time." Cypher checked his notes. "For several years, off and on. Seemed to have formed a friendship with your landlord."

"Bad taste in friends, if you ask me," Theo said.

With one ear on the conversation, Bimmy watched the street activity outside the carriage. She mulled over Theo's invitation. Bimmy Dove, assistant scientist. That had a lovely ring to it.

"Be that as it may, I was wondering if you had ever seen any of Mr. Bottle's visitors."

Theo shook her head. "I can't say that I have. Though if I'm engrossed in an experiment, the President of the United States could come to call on Mr. Bottle and I'd never know it."

It gave Cypher pause to think of Mr. Taft in conversation with one such as Billy Bottle. The image so distracted him that he lost his train of thought.

Bimmy started at the sight of a familiar shape. Wasn't that the girl from the train station? The one selling pickles? She leaned forward for a better view, only to have her vision blocked by a wagon bearing a gigantic cask. After it passed, there was no sign of the girl.

Theo spoke again. "I'm sorry I can't be of more help."

"There is one more thing." Cypher consulted his notes as the cab drew up to the Hippodrome. "Have you spoken with anyone at the theater? Even a few words after rehearsals?"

"I have followed my orders to the T," Theo replied with great sincerity. "I promise. I haven't spoken to a soul."

CHAPTER TWENTY-SIX

Where There's a Will, There's a Way

"How do you know about that?" Divinity squinched her eyes at the triplets, who were hiding behind the dictionary table, across the library. Lilac fought back tears. The tenderhearted triplet was no match for Divinity's icicle glare.

Violet reached for her sister's hand and squeezed, sending along some of her own stalwart spirit with the motion. Emboldened, Lilac took Lavender's hand, passing along the positive energy.

Bolstered by her sisters and with an only slightly trembling voice, Lilac bravely confessed to having overheard Divinity's late-night revelation.

"I said nothing of the sort!" Divinity's mouth wrinkled up as if she'd just eaten an entire lemon. She turned away from the other girls for a moment, pushing books around on the nearest shelf until all the spines lined up just so. "I mean, it was likely a bad dream."

"I tried not to listen. But your voice does carry so." Lilac twisted the hem of her pinafore. "A farm sounds lovely. Though the name is a bit sad: Woebegone's Way."

Divinity's head jerked. "You heard . . . everything?" she asked.

Lilac hung her head, full of remorse.

"And you didn't tell anyone?"

The youngest of the triplets slipped her hands into her pinafore pockets. "Only my sisters."

Divinity paced back and forth on the large rug in front of the grand Dutch-tiled fireplace. She stomped so hard, Lilac feared she would wear a hole right through. "All right. So you know. What are you going to tell Miss Maisie?"

"Why, nothing!" Lilac looked up at the taller Wayward in genuine surprise. "It's not our story to tell. It's yours."

To the triplets' complete and utter shock, a tear bobbed up in Divinity's eye. They had never seen her cry. No one had!

Their soft hearts could not bear such sorrow. The little girls rushed around Divinity, enveloping her in a hug. "It's all right, it's all right," Lavender reassured with gentle pats on the back.

After a moment, Divinity cleared her throat and the circle eased apart, all four Waywards studying their boot toes in embarrassment.

When they had first gathered in the library, Violet had been determined to explain their plan to Divinity, but the moment of tenderness had derailed her.

It was Divinity herself who took the lead. "Why did you bring my—I mean the—farm up at this moment?" she asked.

The triplets exchanged glances. Violet was still so stupefied by the thought of Divinity having feelings like everyone else, that she was speechless. Uncharacteristically, Lavender took the lead. Out poured the whole story—as much as they knew it—from Audie.

"And so you see," Lilac said, completing her recitation, "we *need* a farm. And you *have* a farm—"

"That I don't need," Divinity inserted, folding her arms across her chest. "Or want."

Again, the trio exchanged glances.

"So—" Violet began. This seemed to be going very badly. Audie would be so disappointed in them. They might even be ousted from the Order of Percy! Her lower lip began to quiver.

"So." Divinity retied the strings of her pinafore. "I'll ride the bicycle into town right after lunch and send a telegram informing that lawyer to make all the arrangements." She stood tall in the center of the room. "Tell Audie Woebegone's Way is hers."

CHAPTER TWENTY-SEVEN

The Plan's Afoot

Jamie tugged at the shirt collar he'd been made to wear. His assistant elephant trainer attire had not passed muster with the Shuberts. They sent him straightaway to the wardrobe mistress, who wrangled him into a navy cutaway jacket, black trousers, and white shirt so heavily starched Jamie could barely bend his arms.

"You're a handsome one," she pronounced, setting a black bowler over his thick hair.

No one had ever complimented Jamie Doolan on his appearance before. He snuck a peek in a backstage mirror. He didn't look half bad, even if he said so himself. But it seemed like a lot of fuss just to hand out programs.

He tipped his hat to Baby. "I clean up pretty fine, don't I?"

Baby answered with a snuffle. He stood patiently while Jamie affixed a gigantic blue ribbon around his neck. "What do you think about this nonsense?" Jamie wondered aloud. Because he knew Baby had thoughts. Rich and deep and elephant-like. Jamie had filled his free hours studying those books from Audie. Some mighty interesting stuff in there, all right. Elephants were complicated creatures. Jamie calculated that a person could study them for a lifetime and still have only a thimbleful of knowledge.

"Ready to get to our station?" Jamie reached into his pocket and brought out a large key. He worked it into the lock at Baby's foot and released him from the metal manacle. The welts on Baby's skin pained him as much as if he himself were wounded. That was why he'd signed on with Audie. The girl juggler had no doubts their plan would work. But Jamie was not as certain. Life had taught him to be wary. Even so, he'd thrown his lot in with her and her cat. Jamie would clutch at any straw, do anything—even give up his own freedom—to help Baby.

Jamie clucked his tongue and Baby followed, through the cage doors, out of the basement, and up a ramp to the street. They had a bit of a walk from the theater's rear door to the front entrance, where Baby was to hand out programs to patrons. And there was a stop to be made along the way.

Outside, the young elephant balked at the street commotion—Jamie could only imagine what Baby thought of all the smells. And all the horses and automobiles and people created a racket such as this little one never would hear in his homeland.

"There, Baby. 'Tis all right." Jamie walked backward, leading his charge to the corner of Forty-Third and Sixth. He crooned the words to "Hush Ye, My Bairnie," and would've been hard-pressed to say whether it was to calm Baby or himself.

Minutes passed. And no sign of Audie. His heart sank, but he had to face facts. This was yet another lollipop dream. How could two orphans work wonders? Jamie patted Baby's side, ready to admit defeat.

Then he saw her.

"I was afraid you'd turned chicken," he exclaimed.

Audie set Min down to catch her breath. "My word is my bond," she assured him. "Are we ready to bargain?"

He reached into his pocket. "Here's everything I've got."

She glanced at the bills and coins in Jamie's callused palm. "That *should* be enough." She wiggled her left foot in her boot, hoping she wouldn't have to use the remaining gold coin from her inheritance. But if that was required, that was what she would do. She felt quite certain her parents would approve.

Attired in her Pomegranto costume—the time was fast approaching for the big show—Audie fell in step with Jamie as he led the way, with an elephant and cat padding along behind. The wagon master was at the appointed meeting place with the required equipment. He withheld comment on Audie's appearance but frowned as he counted the money. "This is a little short of what we discussed," he grumbled.

Audie, ever truthful, acknowledged the accuracy of his observation. "There are more important things in this world than gold and silver," she asserted.

The wagon master stared. "Such as?"

"Emerson said, 'Doing well is the result of doing good,'" she replied.

The man continued to stare.

"Ralph Waldo Emerson," Audie clarified.

"Is Ralph going to come up with the difference?" The wagon master appeared to be unmoved by Audie's appeal to his conscience. "I'm not in the charity business, you know."

At that moment an impatient Min jumped to the wagon bed.

"Hey, get away, you scamp!" The wagon master moved to shoo her off. But Min's tail twitched twice, freezing the man's hands in midair. He blinked. Glanced again at the baby elephant and at the money in his hand. "I guess it looks about right, after all." He stuffed the bills and coins into his pocket.

Audie signaled her extreme gratitude to Min, while Jamie stood, dumbfounded. "Shall we continue?" Audie nudged Jamie gently with her elbow.

"What?" He shook his head. "Oh yes." He appeared to bring himself back to the situation at hand. "Give me twenty minutes. Is everything ready?"

"Now or never," the wagon master replied.

Jamie turned to Audie. "Wish me luck."

"You won't need it." She stuck out her hand. "Do stay in touch."

Jamie's mind was already on the next steps, actions that would forever change the course of his life. Houdini might have no trouble vanishing an elephant, but it was another thing altogether to make one truly disappear. The assistant elephant keeper only hoped their plan would work as well in reality as it had seemed to work on paper. He had no desire to go to jail. He became aware of Audie's outstretched hand. "I promise."

After the handshake, Audie brushed her palms together. "That's it, then. I'd best get backstage." Before she had gone two steps, her shadow materialized.

"Whatcha doing?" Daisy turned her infamous squint on the pair.

Jamie gulped. Audie's mind frantically juggled possible answers. But as ever, our girl was truthful. "We're rescuing that elephant," she said. "Baby."

Daisy's hand scrubbed at her nose. "You're doing no such thing."

The coconspirators exchanged glances. "We certainly aim to give it a shot," Audie answered.

"That's crazy," Daisy said.

"There are many who would agree with you," Audie replied pleasantly.

Daisy squinted at them again. "Who owns this here elephant?"

Jamie shoved his hands in his pockets, rattled with nerves. "The time," he reminded Audie.

Again, Audie could be nothing but honest. "Technically, the Shubert brothers."

"Not you?" Squint.

"No." Audie shook her head.

"Sounds like I should call the cops, then." Daisy put her fingers to her mouth, ready to let loose a scalding whistle.

Baby reached out his trunk. Felt around Daisy's shoulders. The pickle seller batted him away.

Audie did so hate to be rude. But every moment was precious, and if they spent much more time squabbling with Daisy, the plan would have no chance at all. She squeezed her hands into fists and waved them threateningly. "I'll be obliged to give you a knuckle sandwich if you don't step out of our way."

Daisy gaped. She choked. Then she burst out laughing. "You

wouldn't know the first thing about fisticuffs," she scoffed, "'cept what you read in a book—"

"That is true," Audie conceded, fists still at the ready.

"Give it a rest." Daisy reached into her pocket and pulled out a sugar cube, which she fed to Baby. "Looks like you could use my help."

CHAPTER TWENTY-EIGHT

Smoke and Mirrors, But Especially Mirrors

"Allow me." The Great Oberon swung his cape over his shoulder and held out his hand to assist Theo down the last few steps from the upstairs dressing room.

"Thank you." Distracted, she tried to hurry by the man. She had much to do before meeting her fellow Pomegrantos for one last run-through.

"Would you like a signed photograph?" Oberon held out an eight-by-ten glossy. He'd made sure that his publicity photos were larger than Houdini's.

Theo hesitated, then took it. "Thank you." But the Great Oberon did not let go of the photo. He tugged it close, thus tugging Theo closer. From his vest pocket, he pulled a watch. He swung it in front of her eyes.

"Do not forget," he said. "You have an important job tonight."

"An important job," Theo echoed, each word flat as a river rock.

"You know exactly what to do?" he pressed.

"The mirrors." She nodded. "Move the mirrors."

"Good girl." He slipped the watch back into his vest, and snapped his fingers. "Break a leg tonight, young lady."

Theo blinked, stretched, yawned. "Oh yes. Thank you, sir." She gave a nod and hurried off to find the rest of her ensemble.

Wurme allowed himself a hearty laugh. To think: In a short time, he would witness Harry Houdini falling flat on his face. And at the ready in the wings would be the man who would not only take Houdini's place on the stage, but would take his place in the world of magic. Wylie Wurme allowed himself several moments to imagine his new and glorious future: audiences with royalty, suites at grand hotels, women in minks eager to buy him dinner. And Houdini would be nothing more than a smashed bug on the windshield of Wurme's new Delaunay-Belleville touring car, ruing the day he had ill-treated Wylie Wurme by rejecting his membership application to the Society of American Magicians.

Revenge was delicious.

CHAPTER TWENTY-NINE

Minutes Until Showtime

Bert's eyes were glued to his pocket watch. Soon, he would dash to the various dressing rooms to shout, "Five minutes, please." The final dash would be to the dressing room of Harry Houdini, calling him out to perform what might be his most fantastic illusion ever.

"Isn't it magical, sir?" one of the young stagehands asked. "Being present to see Mr. Houdini make an entire elephant disappear?"

Moaning, the stage manager flapped his hands at the boy as if trying to make *him* disappear.

"Are you well, sir?" the young man asked.

"As well as can be expected," Bert replied. "Go check on—" He waved his hand deeper backstage, an action that encompassed much instruction.

"A word, Bert?" The Great Oberon appeared at the stage manager's elbow, carrying a large canvas satchel.

"I'm very busy." Bert rubbed his forehead. Who was this? Not the juggler. And not the seal man. He remembered. That audition. "We're about to open the curtain. This isn't the time—"

The Great Oberon smiled. "Well, Bert, my time is nearer at hand than you realize."

"All right, all right, Algernon—"

"Oberon!" Wylie Wurme hadn't quite worked out how he was going to permanently take over that stage name. Apparently, the real Oberon had gone west, seeking his fortune, taking his Asrah Levitation gear with him. That was why Wylie couldn't add that illusion to his repertoire, why he'd had to fake those robberies. Maybe it was Canada that Oberon had set out for. Did it truly matter? He hadn't been heard from in years. After tonight, *he* would be the Great Oberon. And Wylie wouldn't rely on cheap tricks like the Asrah Levitation. He would produce grander and grander illusions. Make an elephant vanish? Posh. That was baby stuff. He would—well, he hadn't actually thought about *what* he would do to surpass Houdini. What was larger than an elephant? A city? Yes, that was it. He, the Great Oberon, would make an entire city disappear! Of course, he wouldn't start with New York. Much too large. What about that burg he'd passed through on the train? Swayzee, Indiana, that was it. He would make Swayzee, Indiana, disappear. *That* was a place no one would miss, or he was no magician.

Wurme continued. "Far be it from me to cast aspersions on a fellow performer." He coughed into his fist. "But it seems to me that this evening Mr. Houdini is promising a great deal more than he can deliver."

"Why would you say that?" Bert sneezed right in Wurme's face. "Pardon me."

"Vanish an elephant?" Wurme's eyes widened. "I mean, really."

Bert vigorously blew his nose. Oh, if he lived to be one hundred, he would never, ever, deal with magicians again. A definite career change was called for, and soon. Maybe he could help his cousin with his dynamite business.

"On the outside chance that Mr. Houdini is not able to fulfill his promises"—Wurme reached into his satchel—"I am most willing to step in." He produced a fistful of handbills.

Bert ignored the sheets presented him. "Nothing will go wrong tonight. Now, in the name of liverwurst, get out of my hair!"

Before the Great Oberon could say more, the young stagehand came running.

"Now what?" Bert tore at his thinning hair like a madman.

"The walrus," the boy said.

"Walrus?" The stage manager grabbed hold of the boy and shook him like a rag doll. "We have no walrus."

Eyes rattling, the stagehand tried to gather his thoughts. It was a creature of the sea, he was certain. Slimy thing, too. And reeked to high heaven. "Seal!" he spat out. "The seal."

Bert sucked in a great breath. "What about it?"

The boy grabbed his sleeve. "You'd just better come along," was all he could manage.

They were both gone in a flash, leaving the Great Oberon standing alone. No matter. After tonight, he would never again be alone. The admiring crowds would press so tightly around him that he'd be imprinted with their buttons. He could wait. It was only a matter of an hour or so before his marvelous dreams would come true.

* * *

Shortly before the Pomegrantos went on, they rehearsed backstage one last time. Bimmy fumbled an easy cascade.

"Are you nervous, chum?" Audie asked.

"A little." Bimmy struggled with whether to tell Audie what she'd been thinking about. Theo's laboratory had been so fascinating. And though Bimmy had never before allowed herself such dreams, the notion of assistant scientist fell on her shoulders like a warm, well-fitting coat. Yet how could she ever part from Audie? Bimmy bit another fingernail down to the quick.

"I too must confess to a case of nerves." Theo pushed her spectacles up on her nose.

"We're going to knock them dead." Audie performed a shower with three small rubber balls. She fumbled at the end. "Well." She shrugged. "At least we'll try."

Cypher paced backstage left. It was one thing to juggle balls; it was another to juggle people. Keeping an eye on Theo and Houdini stretched him thin. And then there were his charges. On top of everything else, whose idea was it that they wear tassels? No man should be made to wear tassels. "I'm not going on," he called over to the girls. "I feel ridiculous."

"Nonsense," Audie replied. Certain schemes revolved around the act going on as planned. Exactly as planned. "A person can do anything once," she encouraged her mentor.

"When you get out on the stage, you won't even notice what

you've got on," Bimmy offered. "I've worn worse costumes than this, but once I began my bit, it didn't matter. Not one iota." She reached out to pat Cypher but pulled back as she took in his expression. "It's not about what we're wearing. It's all about the fantasy we create." She grinned. "Though we may actually have to hypnotize this audience to convince them we're jugglers."

Bimmy did not notice the odd expression on Theo's face at this remark.

"I think you look handsome," Audie proclaimed. "I only wish Beatrice could see you!"

Cypher grimaced.

"Oh, listen!" Audie exclaimed. "The orchestra's warming up."

"It's nearly time." Bimmy double-checked that she had all of her juggling equipment.

"Tassels!" Cypher sighed.

"Everything will be hunky-dory." Audie did several pliés to get limber. "Right, Theo?"

"I think I can safely say this will be an evening of amazements." The girl scientist pushed her glasses up on the bridge of her nose. "Absolute amazements."

CHAPTER THIRTY

Exactly According to Plan

Audie was envious of Bimmy's apparent ease despite the fact they'd just been given their call. The words "Pomegrantos, five minutes!" caused her stomach to perform several loop-de-loops and her knees to turn to gelatin.

"All right there, chum?" Bimmy ran through a series of backcross throws.

Audie daren't watch the balls as they went behind Bimmy's back and over her shoulder, around and around without a fumble. The motion made her feel seasick. "I'm hunky-dory." She swallowed hard. "Remember?" Then she busied herself with tightening the lacing on her costume, so as not to let Bimmy see what a wreck she was. Stopping kidnappers was a far sight easier than acting onstage!

"Two minutes," Bert whispered.

Audie couldn't be certain, but she thought she might have heard Cypher gulp. Could his nerves be frazzled, too? Cypher?

"It seems everything will go according to plan." Theo bounced up and down on her toes.

"At this moment," Audie confessed, "I am more worried about *our* performance than Mr. Houdini's."

"We can't let down our guard," Cypher cautioned. "Not until the elephant has vanished."

"Yes," agreed Theo.

Audie bent to tie her slipper, hiding her face. "Of course," she said.

"And on!" Bert pointed to the foursome.

"Break a nose!" Theo called gaily.

"Leg!" Bimmy cried in panic. "It's break a *leg*!"

Their musical cue pulled them through the curtain. Once out front, the stage lights froze Audie in place.

"Chum," Bimmy urged. "Juggle!"

After the initial shock, Audie realized the bright lights were her friends, preventing her from seeing any one of the five-thousand-odd spectators. She could pretend it was just her, Bimmy, Theo, and Cypher. At this realization, she threw herself into the performance. Cypher and Bimmy had the trickier moves of the foursome, but Bimmy had choreographed some bits for Theo and Audie that were flashy enough to look challenging.

All four wore ebullient smiles as balls sailed up and around, back and forth, to and fro. Cypher garnered grand applause for the routine where he juggled three heavy wooden clubs. Bimmy added some acrobatics to her portion, and Audie and Theo did their utmost not to bobble anything. Then, *"Zut!"* called Cypher, and he and Bimmy performed a most complex double juggling routine, which began with Cypher appearing to throw a club smack at Bimmy's head. She caught it and cartwheeled, and the crowd cheered. It was a stunning finale.

Bert couldn't have been more surprised at it, well deserving of its one curtain call. Miracles did happen, it seemed. Maybe he'd stay in the theater business after all. At least for another week.

"Bravo!" Bert patted them each on the back as they ran offstage, panting and glowing with exertion.

"Not bad." The Great Oberon pulled a bouquet of paper flowers from his sleeve, which he presented to Theo. "But soon you will see the best."

"Yes," agreed Bimmy. "Mr. Houdini."

"That's not what I meant." Oberon smiled mysteriously. He swirled his cape around his shoulder. "Step this way. We'll have the best view from here."

Everyone backstage quieted, vying for prime viewing spots as the orchestra played the dramatic first notes of the musical introduction for Mr. Houdini. Even Herring the seal quieted his barking to observe a master at work.

Houdini strode to the center of the stage. His beeswaxed hair glistened in the spotlights. He wore no cape, but was simply and elegantly attired in a crisp white collared shirt under a black morning coat with velvet lapels.

Audie's breath caught as he began to speak.

"Laadies and gintlemen!" Houdini somehow cast the words out over the crowd so that every single one of the five thousand in attendance could hear plain as day. "Laadies and gintlemen!"

As she watched, he transformed himself from a short man with a shy smile and soft eyes into a force to be reckoned with. He seemed to have grown several feet taller and those eyes burned from within, fueled by some incredible passion. It was beyond remarkable. No matter what happened with the illusion, Mr. Houdini convinced Audie of one fact: Nothing was as magical as the human imagination.

"Ah." Houdini waved his arm. "My friend has arrived."

An enormous collective breath was held as Jennie, all seven thousand pounds of her, soldiered onto the stage. She wore an enormous bow around her neck, a feature that only served to accentuate her size. Compared to the master magician, she seemed like Jack's giant. He remained poised in the spotlight, unflinching as the elephant lumbered closer. When she was nearly upon the compact man, she paused. Swayed.

"Well, hello, Jennie!" Mr. Houdini reached into his pocket and produced lumps of sugar. The elephant inhaled them and the crowd roared its appreciation. Mr. Houdini continued. "Gracious friends, allow me to introduce Jennie, the world's only vanishing elephant."

Jennie raised her trunk to greet those who had come to watch her disappear. That trunk then lowered, feeling around the magician, searching for more treats.

"Oh, dear Jennie." Houdini turned out his pockets. "That's all the sugar I have."

The enormous elephant trumpeted. The tremendous sound reverberated through Audie, nearly knocking her off balance. Then Jennie rose up on her hind legs, and three and a half tons of elephant towered over the magician. A woman in the audience screamed.

"Now, now, Jennie." Houdini winked, a gesture that should only have been visible to those audience members in the first few rows but was somehow seen even in the cheap seats. "You must watch your girlish figure."

The crowd roared again. Houdini had them in his complete power. It was as if he had cast a spell. He *had* cast a spell, Audie realized. It was called showmanship.

Still, Audie held her breath. The elephant was so large and the magician so small. Finally, Jennie lowered to all fours.

Houdini gestured to the wings and eight stagehands appeared, pulling with them an enormous, garishly painted box, sitting atop a flat wagon propelled by four equally enormous wheels. The music rumbled and roared, setting hearts racing throughout the theater.

Audie grabbed Bimmy's hand. "This is so exciting!" She glanced over to where Theo had been standing. That young English acrobat stood in her place. Surely she wasn't going to miss this?

"Where's Theo?" Audie whispered.

Bimmy looked around. "She was here just a moment ago."

"Maybe Mr. Houdini needed her help with something during the act."

"That must be it." Bimmy turned her attention back to the stage. "Yes, there she is."

Theo, still clad in her Pomegranto costume, had made her way to one group of the stagehands. The men seemed confused, murmuring among themselves.

Houdini, hearing the noise, turned. Spied Theo. If he was shocked to see her there, he gave no sign of it.

"Ah, my associate felt the need to show you good folks that there is nothing suspicious about this illusion." He waved grandly at Theo, indicating for her to enter the box.

Theo climbed the ramp, pointing her toes daintily with each step.

"I don't think this was part of the plan." Cypher nervously tapped a juggling club against his palm.

"But Houdini doesn't seem surprised," Audie observed.

Bimmy arched an eyebrow. "The show must go on, whether he's surprised or not."

"I'm having a grand time." The Great Oberon chuckled. "Quite the performance."

Audie nodded uneasily. Why was the Great Oberon in such good spirits? He didn't seem the type to wish others well.

Theo had reached the end of the ramp, and now, with much gesturing and curtsying, was showing off the inside of the painted box.

"No false bottom," Houdini called out. "No back door. No trickery!"

Thunderous applause ricocheted off the Hippodrome's walls.

Audie wasn't certain, but she thought she heard Oberon say, "No trickery indeed."

Theo performed a pirouette as she skipped down the ramp, then took a deep bow before dance-walking offstage into the wings. The audience, bursting with anticipation, stamped their feet.

Houdini clapped three times, the signal for the trainer to send Jennie up the ramp into the very box Theo had just vacated. As music thrummed throughout the theater, the elephant was situated inside.

Doors at the front of the box were closed. Locked. The crowd cheered. The stagehands slowly, slowly rotated the box to reconfirm there was no rear exit.

"Bid farewell, ladies and gentleman, to our darling Jennie!" Houdini raised his hand. A drumroll tattooed a pounding rhythm. The theater grew quiet as a tomb. An eternity passed and yet it was only moments.

Houdini signaled again, and the stagehands flung open the front door of the box.

It was completely empty.

"NOOOOO!" cried Oberon.

Houdini basked in the spotlight's glow, revolving in a triumphant and slow circle. The crowd flew to its feet, chanting, "Hoo-di-ni! Hoo-di-ni! Hoo-di-ni!"

Backstage, Bert was attempting to restrain Oberon, who was flinging himself this way and that, shouting out words that, quite honestly, dear reader, should not reach young ladies' ears.

Houdini was now speaking to the audience, but Audie couldn't hear, not over the Great Oberon's tantrum. She edged away from the wings, confused about her course of action. In the moment of Houdini's triumph, she was to have been making her way to the back alley.

"You!" Oberon, fairly foaming at the mouth, pointed at Theo. "You, you!"

Theo approached the imposter magician and removed another string from her finger. "There's a job well done," she said.

"I don't understand," Oberon sputtered. "You were supposed to shift the mirrors."

Theo smiled. "Oh, surely, Mr. Wylie Wurme, as a master hypnotist, you of all people would know that a person cannot be hypnotized into doing something she wouldn't ordinarily do." She adjusted her spectacles on her nose. "And I certainly wouldn't sabotage Mr. Houdini's act."

Enraged, the phony Oberon broke free from Bert. He lunged at Theo, grabbed her, and, in a shocking instant, drew out a knife. Audie cried out as he placed it at Theo's throat. "No! No!"

Houdini stepped backstage, preparing for his first curtain call, completely oblivious to the danger Theo was in. He parted the curtains to accept another round of applause.

Wurme dragged Theo toward the rear door. "Don't any of you move," he threatened. "Not if you want to see her alive again."

At that moment, Min appeared, along with a pickle peddler, both come looking for Audie, who was late for a certain rendezvous. *"Mer-row,"* she said.

"If you think that's wise, Min," Audie replied. "Cypher, Bimmy! *Zut!*" She motioned for Daisy to snatch up Herring's ball and throw it to Bimmy, which she did at the exact moment Cypher let fly his heavy club.

Wurme released Theo to protect his head from the wooden missile. He scrambled away, screaming in pain as Min latched on to his back, her claws digging deeper and deeper.

In one smooth motion, Bimmy caught and then swung Herring's ball, bowling Wurme off his feet.

Still oblivious, Houdini took his fourth curtain call, exhilarated by the illusion's success. Everything had gone so smoothly. Perfectly according to plan. He truly was the greatest magician in the world.

Bert and Cypher pulled Wurme to his feet. "Call the police," Bert said. "And let's get this phony behind bars where he belongs."

Wurme started to struggle but gave it up when he saw Billy Bottle approach from stage left, waving a bounced check that was to have been in payment for certain information. Billy looked most perturbed. From stage right approached two thugs, looking equally unhappy. They'd been sent by their boss to collect on a rather large bet Wurme had placed, certain that Houdini's Vanishing Elephant illusion would be a bust. Given the turn of events, Wurme was more than content to go with the police.

Faces flushed, Cypher and Bimmy congratulated each other on their role in Wurme's arrest. Houdini approached them after his tenth, and final, curtain call, nearly floating with the thrill of success.

"Oh, I must thank Theo," he said. "Where is she?"

"Right over—" Bimmy pointed to the spot where just a moment ago Theo had undergone questioning by the police. "I don't see her."

"And where's Audie?" Cypher's heart sank. Saving Theo meant little if harm had come to his charge. His friend.

"Mr. Cypher?" Archibald Leach, one of the English acrobats, came running up. He handed Cypher a sealed note, which was quickly opened. Bits of string, like confetti, fell out. "It's from Theo," Cypher said, and he began to read aloud. "'I won't need these anymore as I have found the perfect assistant. When things settle down, I will send an address should you care to come visit.'"

"Oh!" A dreadful realization came over Bimmy. This explained why Audie had been so secretive. *She* had accepted the position as Theo's assistant! Bimmy explained her theory to Cypher, doing her best to hide her double disappointment that Audie would leave her and that she herself had lost the opportunity to be Theo's right-hand girl.

"Your reasoning is sound," Cypher agreed. "But I do not concur with your conclusion. Audie would never leave the Waywards. She is far too loyal."

"You two look as if you've lost your best friends and some cash," Houdini said. "Cheer up! The Vanishing Elephant illusion was a huge success." The Brothers Shubert had already approached him with quite a lucrative contract to perform it weekly over the next few months.

"I regret to inform you that Theo is gone." Cypher showed Houdini the note.

"I will miss the odd thing," said the great magician. "But she held up her end of the bargain and I wish her well." He frowned when he saw that his words did not lift their spirits. "Perhaps I can help." He whistled for Bobby, who flew to his master. "Fetch my wand!"

"Oh, you don't need to do any more magic for us," Bimmy said. There was no trick that could fix what was wrong. How was she going to manage without her dearest chum?

"We'd best be going." Cypher began unlacing his costume. He had to find Audie! Beatrice would never forgive him if he returned to Miss Maisie's without her.

Bobby trotted back, a black wand in his mouth. Houdini took it from the terrier. "Humor me," he said.

"A trick would be very nice," Bimmy answered politely.

Cypher sighed.

Houdini waved his wand toward a portion of the heavy burgundy stage curtain. "Abracadabra! Bees and bonnets!"

A flash of light. Then white smoke.

"Audie!" Bimmy ran to her friend. "You didn't leave."

Cypher wanted to swoop the Wayward orphan up in his arms, he was that overjoyed to see her. But he managed to control himself. "Bimmy thought you'd gone off to be Theo's assistant," he said.

"Bees and bonnets," Audie replied. "Why would you think that? I've already got the best job in the whole wide world." She returned Bimmy's enthusiastic hug.

"Well, where were you?" Bimmy asked. "Did you miss all the excitement?"

Audie's smile was an apt imitation of the Mona Lisa's. Small and mysterious. "Oh, I don't think I missed it *all*," she assured her best friend.

"And here's Min!" Bimmy cheered. "Now our party's complete."

Cypher rubbed his forehead. Despite all of his efforts, he had ended up in charge of two children and a cat. He smiled. *C'est la vie!*

Min carried something in her mouth. "Where did you get that blue ribbon, you silly cat?" Bimmy asked.

Min wisely chose not to answer.

From the depths of the Hippodrome stormed Helmut, shouting for Bert. He slid to a halt when he saw Houdini. "I don't know what you're up to," he said, fairly spitting nails. "But your illusion really did vanish an elephant."

"Of course it did." Houdini's chest went out. "It was rather a good trick, too. Jennie was a trouper. I'll give her an extra handful of sugar cubes tomorrow."

Helmut stomped his foot like a spoiled child. "I'm not talking about Jennie!" Now his hands formed fists at his sides. "I'm talking about Baby. The darned punk has disappeared."

"My goodness," Audie exclaimed, eyes wide, hiding the blue ribbon behind her back. "That seems impossible." Then she acknowledged Mr. Houdini. "Impossible except for someone as talented as you."

Houdini accepted the compliment with a bow.

Cypher's appraising look was caught by Helmut. He glared at Audie. "If you know anything—" His voice carried a threat. Cypher moved in to protect Audie, but Helmut was interrupted by a grip, holding out an envelope.

"I found this pinned to a rope back there," he said. "Addressed to you."

Helmut ripped the envelope open and pulled out a bill of sale for one male baby elephant. It had been stamped "Paid in Full." But in front of the word *Paid*, someone had written in *Re*. He read it aloud: "'Re-Paid in Full.' What does that mean?"

"That looks like quite a lot of money," Audie observed.

Helmut counted it out. "Fifteen hundred dollars."

"Astonishing," said Audie.

"I wonder—" Houdini began.

"What?" Helmut snapped. "Do you know something more about this?"

Audie cleared her throat, attempting to send a mental message to the world-famous magician.

"I meant, I wonder," Houdini continued, "if the young ladies would do me the honor of their presence at my home. Mrs. Houdini promises a lovely tea."

Audie slipped her arm through Bimmy's and then addressed Cypher. "Shall we go? All this commotion has me absolutely famished."

CHAPTER THIRTY-ONE

Keys to the Case

Mr. Houdini gathered them all into his grand parlor at West 113th Street. A fire crackled in the fireplace, and Mrs. Houdini—"Call me Bess!"—had set out plates of small sandwiches and cookies. Audie sampled one of each, sharing bites with Bobby and Min.

"So, my darling," Mrs. Houdini, *Bess*, began. "Your grand illusion was even grander than initially planned." She patted her lap and Bobby leapt into it. She did not seem to mind the tan hairs the dog was shedding all over her black velveteen skirt.

"I guess I'm more powerful than even I imagined." Mr. Houdini threw his head back and barked a laugh. "I have apparently disappeared an assistant elephant keeper, a scientific genius, and one young elephant."

Audie attempted to hide her reaction to this observation by reaching for a dainty chintz teacup and sipping thoughtfully.

"Do they need finding?" Cypher cast a curious glance Audie's way. "I have an idea of where I might start."

Audie coughed.

"No, no." Houdini shook his leonine head. "No need."

Audie could not help but admire the way the flames reflected off the magician's dark, wavy hair.

He continued. "After all, Helmut was provided with funds sufficient to compensate the Shuberts for their investment in Baby." Though he would never speak this thought aloud, Houdini did not think it a coincidence that the envelope had contained fifteen hundred dollars, the exact amount he had paid Theo Quinn for designing the Vanishing Elephant illusion.

"And do the Shuberts feel adequately reimbursed?" Cypher inquired.

"They have been overcome with remorse about purchasing the baby elephant in the first place," Houdini said. "Though such a change of heart seems quite unlike them."

Min paused in her toilette and *mer-row*ed. Audie had a fairly clear notion of the source of the Shuberts' changes of heart. "Good puss," she said, sharing a chunk of Jarlsberg with Min.

"Still," said Cypher, "there are many mysteries yet unsolved with this case." He wasn't sure how Mr. Pinkerton was going to react.

"Mysteries are the essence of life!" Houdini smiled warmly at Audie, who, though deeply familiar with the details of the case of the vanishing baby elephant, was as yet unaware of an important bit of information.

There had been a third envelope left behind. Mysteriously, magically, Houdini had found it tucked under Bobby's collar. The enclosed letter vowed to take certain secrets to the grave, as long as its writer was allowed to start a new life. Said letter had been signed with initials only: TQ.

"It would be such a relief if the Shuberts didn't get another one," Bimmy said. "Elephant, I mean."

Audie had engaged in quite the stern discourse with herself on this very topic. Saving Baby would not prevent the capture and mistreatment of other elephants. But one had to start somewhere, didn't one? "Wouldn't it be wonderful if all wild creatures were allowed to remain wild?"

"Our little friend is quite the philosopher," Houdini commented to Cypher.

"Oh, but I am very poorly read on *that* topic," Audie demurred. "I promise that philosophy shall be one of the first subjects I study when I arrive home." *Home*. The word was as sweet on her lips as one of Beatrice's *canelés*. New York had proved a thrilling adventure, but now that Baby was safe, and their other mission successfully, though unconventionally, discharged, her thoughts turned toward Miss Maisie's School and her fellow Waywards.

"We'll start for Swayzee soon." Cypher seemed to grasp Audie's longing.

"I hope not too soon," Houdini said. "I'm treating you all to front-row seats at tomorrow night's show." The mahogany grandfather clock chimed the hour of midnight. "Or rather, this evening's show."

"Might we take a rain check on that kind offer?" Audie enjoyed the combined look of surprise and dismay on Bimmy's face. She could almost read her friend's mind: *Are you mad? How could you turn down such an invitation?*

"I thought we weren't to leave for another day." Bimmy found herself feeling quite peevish at her dear friend. After all, when again in their Wayward lives would they have the opportunity to see the great Houdini perform? And front-row seats at that.

Audie pressed her lips together, barely able to keep the good news to herself any longer. "That is true. But you have plans. Other plans. Pressing plans."

"I do?" Bimmy looked completely bewildered.

Cypher stifled a yawn. "We must take our leave."

Audie rose from her seat. "Thank you so much for the tour of your lovely home and for the delicious hors d'oeuvres." She curtsied to the Houdinis. Harry and Bess. And Bobby.

Cypher and Bimmy also expressed their gratitude for the Houdini hospitality.

"I can't thank *you* all enough." Mr. Houdini reached for Bimmy's ear. "Why, look what I've found!" A small blue box appeared in his hand. He repeated the same feat with Audie. Upon opening the boxes, the girls discovered tiny sterling silver keys, imprinted on each stem with *T & Co.* in delicate script. Each key dangling from a glittering silver chain. Mr. Houdini winked. "A souvenir to remind you of the Greatest Escape Artist in the World."

"As if we could ever forget you!" Audie promptly donned the sweet souvenir from Mr. Tiffany's store.

Bimmy hesitated. Around her neck was hanging the locket given her by her mother, a memento of the first time she'd performed in the Family Dove act, sans net. It was a treasure she never, ever removed, not even while bathing. Bimmy dreaded offending the great magician so she lifted the chain from the blue box. It was shorter than Audie's. "A bracelet," she exclaimed, doubly grateful.

"A magician is trained to notice things." Mr. Houdini bowed.

Bimmy kissed his cheek. She would never forget this kindness.

As coats were gathered and movements made toward leaving, Bobby hopped down from Mrs. Houdini's lap. Bess opened her arms and gave each girl a hug. "You've always a place to stay when you come to New York," she whispered in Audie's ear. "You and your friend. You and any of your friends."

Arm in arm, the Houdinis escorted their guests to the front door. "And now for my final trick of the evening!" Houdini waved his handkerchief. "I will make three lovely people disappear!"

Audie glanced down the hall behind the magician. "Three people and one cat," she added, smiling as Min led Bobby on a scrabbling chase through the house. She had no worries for Min's safety, though she was fretful about Bobby's pride.

CHAPTER THIRTY-TWO

A Bit of Magic for Bimmy

The next evening, Cypher opened the door so the girls could exit the taxicab. "Here we are," he said.

"But where is here?" Bimmy stepped onto the sidewalk. "And why?"

"Be patient." Audie took Bimmy's hand and led her through the front door of the Hotel Belleclaire and into the toasty-warm lobby, bustling with an assortment of performers from a very particular circus brought across the Atlantic to celebrate the birthday of one of John D. Rockefeller's grandchildren. The tyke was mad for the big top, and Mr. Rockefeller was mad to keep his grandchildren happy. The expense of transporting the circus and a goodly portion of its performers for one night's entertainment was nothing to the richest man in the world.

In the lobby, the air was charged with anticipation, as if something grand was in the works, something more than a birthday party.

Bimmy's face was a question mark for a full minute as she stood at the edge of the crowded room. Then two figures gracefully stepped through the archway from the elevators.

"Mama!" She flew to the first of the figures. "Papa!"

Audie's joy for her friend leaked out both eyes. Mr. and Mrs. Dove could not stop hugging and kissing their beloved daughter. Audie was completely satisfied. All the subterfuge had been worthwhile, even though Bimmy and her mother and father would have but one evening together. It was heartwarming to see them all so happy. To see Bimmy so happy. Our Audie was such a gracious soul that she didn't for a moment begrudge Bimmy what she herself would never have: a family reunion. After a glance at Cypher, Audie removed a second handkerchief from her pocket. "It looks like you could use this," she said.

"This city is so dirty." He dabbed at his eyes. "All that ash and soot."

They watched the tender scene a few moments more.

"Shall we leave them to get reacquainted?" Audie suggested. "I'm famished." She led the way back to the waiting cab and provided the driver with directions she'd gleaned from a certain steely-eyed purveyor of pickles. The long and bumpy ride was well worth the look on Cypher's face when he opened the door to an out-of-theway and uniquely ethnic restaurant and was ambushed by the scents of cardamom and turmeric and ginger.

The owner greeted them warmly in Farsi. Cypher beamed as they were led to a table in a quiet corner.

After their lovely many-coursed meal—Audie was particularly fond of the *morgh polou*—and on the cab ride to pick up Bimmy,

Cypher thanked Audie over and over for finding the Persian restaurant.

"It was lovely, wasn't it?" she asked. "Though I think I do prefer Beatrice's *baghlava*." She sighed. "I can't wait to get home to her. Can you?"

Cypher made no answer, and it was too dark for Audie to see him blush.

CHAPTER THIRTY-THREE

A Knock at the Door

Audie entertained Miss Maisie, Beatrice, Cook, and the Waywards with a card trick Mr. Houdini had taught her. They were most amazed at her ability to predict which card they selected.

"Why would anyone ever need to travel to town to see a show?" exclaimed Cook. "Not when our own Audie can prestidigitate with the best of them!"

"Mais oui!" agreed Beatrice.

Audie decided not to dash their illusions about her talents by revealing the secrets she'd learned from the great magician.

"And don't forget Bimmy's juggling prowess," Violet added.

"Say, maybe we could put on a variety show of our own." Audie shuffled the deck of cards. "Raise money for a good cause."

"Our chocolate supply *is* running low," Miss Maisie commented. "That would be a good cause."

"Or maybe the Circus Orphans Society," suggested Audie, tactfully refraining from any comment on Miss Maisie's self-concern.

"Charity begins at home." Miss Maisie pressed her point while fiddling with the butterfly brooch pinned to her bodice.

"I like the idea of helping the Circus Orphans," said Bimmy.

"You would," Divinity interjected before popping a madeleine into her mouth. She chewed and swallowed. "Actually, I like the idea of helping the Circus Orphans, too."

"That's the spirit!" Audie encouraged. Divinity's actions had certainly revealed that old dogs could learn new tricks. But Audie, Bimmy, and the triplets had been sworn to secrecy; they were never to reveal a word about Divinity's generous gift. It seemed a shame, but Audie would honor the eldest Wayward's wishes.

At that moment, the bonging of chimes reached them from the front hall. "We'll answer it," the triplets called. Violet, the spunkiest of the three, reached the door first and pulled it open.

A complete stranger stood there. A complete stranger, yet someone whose face was familiar to each of the triplets, it having been featured prominently in many national newspapers.

It took Violet an instant to put two and two together. She whispered in Lilac's ear, who whispered in Lavender's, who, upon hearing, skidded down the great hall back to the kitchen.

"Audie!" she called, barely able to contain her excitement. "There's someone here to see you."

Author's Note

Had I known that the terrific folks at Scholastic would want a second story about Audacity Jones, I would never have ended the first book where I did, implying that the world-famous magician Harry Houdini would be part of Audie's next adventure. Let this be a lesson to you: Always do your research! You see, *Audacity Jones to the Rescue* is set in the first month of 1910. It would seem logical that her next story would take place shortly after that. However, 1910 found our dear Mr. Houdini pursuing his passion for aviation . . . in Australia. I was sick at heart when I realized this, as there seemed no feasible way to get Audie down under. Further, today's kids, if they know Houdini at all, know him as an escape artist, not an aviator. All was lost.

But as Audie herself says, "If it's not splendid, it's not the end." After I panicked and cried on her shoulder, my gifted editor, Lisa Sandell, suggested giving myself permission to turn down the volume on the history portion of Audie's escapades. It was brilliant advice, freeing me to focus on fun rather than facts. To borrow from Harry himself, "My brain is the key that sets me free."

I allowed my imagination to be the key to unlock the story you're holding in your hand. You will notice there are no dates mentioned, though I am *imagining* 1910 New York City, with its pushcarts, the Sixth Avenue El, and the Hippodrome. These are all elements of that time period's scenery, as were the Hotel Evelyn (which truly was where many vaudevillians stayed) and the Hotel Belleclaire.

A bit about vaudeville: While motion pictures did lead to the virtual demise of this form of entertainment, much silver-screen talent was drawn from vaudeville's stage. Archibald Leach actually was part of an English comic acrobatic team, though he is better known by his stage name, Cary Grant. You may not recognize any of these names, but I bet your grandparents will: Charlie Chaplin, Ed Wynn, and Bert Lahr (the Cowardly Lion in the 1939 film *The Wizard of Oz*) are all movie stars who got their beginnings in vaudeville. Though the world of theater did in many ways reflect societal attitudes, I like to think that Bimmy would have been welcomed at the Hippodrome, a place where one's abilities were what counted, not race, religion, or sex. That belief stems from my research, exemplified by an anecdote from *No Applause—Just Throw Money: The Book that Made Vaudeville Famous* by Trav S.D., which reports that when, in 1911, the entire cast of Ziegfeld Follies threatened to walk out rather than appear with the African-American performer Bert Williams, Flo Ziegfeld reportedly said, "Go if you want to. I can replace every one of you, except the man you want me to fire" (page 11).

It's hard to imagine making an elephant disappear. But Harry Houdini really did accomplish that feat, at least once. I couldn't verify if he performed the illusion more times than that; reports vary. But I was able to confirm that he had help from fellow illusionist Charles Morritt, an Englishman who had created a successful vanishing *donkey* illusion. When Houdini was seeking a respite from his physically demanding escape tricks, he looked Morritt up and they concocted a plan to vanish an even larger creature. Morritt evidently designed the illusion, which was first performed at the Hippodrome on January 7, 1918. Houdini did indeed make Jennie disappear, but the audience was not as enthralled as I describe in Chapter Thirty. This was mainly because the theater was so enormous, very few people could see what was happening. But Jennie did vanish that evening (temporarily). And though both men took the secrets of this trick to their graves, Jim Steinmeyer has written a fascinating book on the topic, *Hiding the Elephant*.

Since this is my story (and Audie's!) to tell, I decided to replace Charles Morritt with my own scientifically inclined assistant to the great Houdini, Theodora Quinn. I created her as a way to honor the many women who have contributed to all facets of the arts and sciences, but have never received recognition for their efforts.

And, finally: Captive baby elephants were called punks in this time period, and training techniques were cruel. To my knowledge, there were no elephant sanctuaries in the United States in the 1900s. But I wish there had been. A portion of my author's royalties for this book will be donated to The Elephant Sanctuary in Hohenwald, Tennessee.

Acknowledgments

Most of my adventures take place on the page, and none of them would happen without some wonderful and generous people. My cousin Shawn O'Donnell, amateur magician and restaurateur extraordinaire, opened his magic library to me, sharing wonderful tomes, old and new, including the book on sleight of hand that Audie takes on her journey. The Bowery Boys (www.boweryboys history.com) transported me to the New York of the early 1900s; beware of tuning in to their podcasts because they are extremely addictive. Silver Sister Jennifer Holm jumped in to help with some New York City historical research, as did Pamela Ryan and Laurel Snyder (I think they may have been procrastinating instead of writing).

I am blessed with a family that makes me laugh and brings unending joy. Esme, Audrey, Eli, and babies-to-be remind me what it's like to be a kid, and also remind me to take time to act like one once in a while (who ever thought Grandma Kirby would go to a video arcade?). I am one lucky mom to have Quinn and Matt,

Tyler and Nicole in my life; thanks, all. And Neil: I owe you big time for everything, including all the Winston-sitting.

I am grateful to be part of a talented and caring community of writers, without whom I would lose heart. Special thanks to Karen Cushman, Mary Nethery, and the Butterfly Sisters (Susan Hill Long, Barbara O'Connor, and Augusta Scattergood). Fist bump.

I have gotten my agent, Jill Grinberg, into so many tight corners, yet she does nothing but smile and say it will all work out; she may have inspired Audie's basic life philosophy. Katelyn Detweler, Cheryl Pientka, and Denise St. Pierre all have Jill's back and thus mine. Special thanks to Eva Beller, Jill's mother-in-law, for help with the Yiddish words.

My Scholastic family supports me in so many ways; I can't believe my luck. Huge thanks to: Jennifer Abbots, Julie Amitie, Lori Benton, Ellie Berger, Bess Braswell, Michelle Campbell, Caitlin Friedman, Antonio Gonzalez, Rachel Feld, Emily Heddleson, Lindsey Johnson, David Levithan, Christine Reedy, Dick Robinson, Lizette Serrano, Tracy van Straaten; Olivia Valcarce; Alan Boyko, Janet Speakman, Robin Hoffman, and the whole Book Fair gang. Thank you, Carol Ly and Brandon Dorman, for another irresistible cover. And my darling editor, Lisa Sandell, deserves an unending supply of chocolate and adult beverages for putting up with me.

As always, readers, I am honored that you would spend time with my books. *Merci!*

HAVE YOU READ AUDACITY'S FIRST ADVENTURE?

NEWBERY HONOR AUTHOR
Kirby Larson
AUDACITY JONES
TO THE RESCUE
SCHOLASTIC

KIRBY LARSON

CODE
WORD
COURAGE

A WWII Navajo Code Talker and a lonely young girl—
can a stray dog save them both?

Don't miss
Code Word Courage
by Kirby Larson!

Here's a sneak peek . . .

The dog did not want to leave the vehicle. Did not want to follow the man. But the rope prevented any other option.

"Pa!" a voice cried from the backseat. "Pa! Don't. Please don't!"

The dog whined to hear his boy so upset. As soon as the man loosened the rope from his neck, he scrambled to return to the car.

The man raised his arm. Hollered. "Git." He pelted the dog with rocks scooped up from the highway shoulder.

Too many of the sharp edges found their marks. And then a large stone cracked something in his side. Try as he might, the dog could no longer stand his ground. Panting to ease the pain, he limped out of range.

A door slammed, then the vehicle sped down the highway. The dog struggled to follow. But his legs gave way and he collapsed in the dirt. He didn't try to get up again.

Without his boy, there was no point.

When WWII comes to the homefront, these kids and their dogs will have to be brave...

The Dogs of World War II Novels
By Newbery Honor Author Kirby Larson